MAGIC QUILTS

By The Slice

BETHANY S. REYNOLDS

American Quilter's Society
P. O. Box 3290 • Paducah, KY 42002-3290
www.AQSquilts.com

Located in Paducah, Kentucky, the American Quilter's Society (AQS) is dedicated to promoting the accomplishments of today's quilters. Through its publications and events, AQS strives to honor today's quiltmakers and their work and to inspire future creativity and innovation in quiltmaking.

EDITOR: BARBARA SMITH
GRAPHIC DESIGN: ELAINE WILSON
HOW-TO ILLUSTRATIONS: BETHANY S. REYNOLDS
COVER DESIGN: MICHAEL BUCKINGHAM
QUILT PHOTOGRAPHY: CHARLES R. LYNCH
HOW-TO PHOTOGRAPHY: WILLIAM W. REYNOLDS

Library of Congress Cataloging-in-Publication Data
Reynolds, Bethany S.
    Magic quilts by the slice / Bethany S. Reynolds
        p. cm.
        ISBN 1-57432-820-4
1. Patchwork--Patterns.   2. Quilting.   3. Rotary cutting.   4. Fans in
art.   I. Title.
    TT835.R45897   2003
    746.46'041--dc21

                        2003003825

Additional copies of this book may be ordered from the American Quilter's Society, PO Box 3290, Paducah, KY 42002-3290; 800-626-5420 (orders only please); or online at www.AQSquilt.com. For all other inquiries, call 270-898-7903.

dedication

For two of my favorite fans…
my mom, Kathryn Suminsby,
and my bonus mom, Claire Reynolds.

FRIENDSHIP FANS, 35" x 48", quilt instructions begin on page 82.

acknowledgments

The staff at the American Quilter's Society has my continued admiration and gratitude. Working with these dedicated professionals is an author's dream.

I am grateful to Ann Czompo and to my fan-class students, including my online students at quiltuniversity.com, for helping me test the techniques and sharing their enthusiasm. Special thanks go to Jo Ann Cooper, Dottie Lankard, and Sandy Curran for sharing their unique fan quilts; and to Eleanor Carlise, whose embroidery talents shine in REDWORK RIBBONS.

Thanks to Pfaff American Sales for letting me use one of their excellent machines to piece and quilt my samples. I also thank the manufacturers who contributed materials for the quilts in this book, including Benartex; P&B Textiles; Hi-Fashion Fabrics, Inc.; Robert Kaufman Co.; Hoffman California Fabrics; RJR Fabrics; Moda Fabrics; Superior Threads; and J.T. Trading Corporation.

And my most heartfelt thanks goes to my husband, Bill, who devoted many hours to the how-to photography, in addition to picking up more than his share of the household chores so I could quilt and write; and to my son, Sam, for all the walks and hugs.

contents

introduction

The first time I pieced fan wedges from a stack of identical layers left over from another project, I was hooked. This is too easy, I thought. Five straight seams and the fan unit was complete—no points to match, no centers to fuss over! Since I'm not really fond of curved piecing, I opted for a simple bias finish, learned in my dressmaking days, then straight-stitched the fan to the background square, hiding the stitching in the seam line. That first experiment led to a design for my book, *Stack-n-Whackier Quilts* (AQS, 2002).

I knew I wasn't done, though. This was too much fun, and there were so many possibilities to explore! I began to play "What If...," a game familiar to many quilters and the source of most of my designs.

First, there were so many different ways to make the blocks. What if I used a single bias edge, instead of the double bias method I'd been using? (Aha! I liked it better!) What if I used fusible bias tape or rick-rack? Pointed fans are an old standard, so that was a "must-try." That led to scalloped wedges, so familiar on Dresden Plate designs. Many, many blocks later, I had worked out techniques to make all of these variations and more. Part One details these

methods. Try a few of them or try them all. These techniques are interchangeable, so you can pick your favorites for your own projects.

All of these beautiful blocks called for simple but versatile settings. What if I repeated the fan base quarter-circles in the cornerstones? What if I made the circles appear to float over the border? What if I set the fans on triangles or diamonds instead of squares? Part Two includes projects based on these ideas and others. Throughout the project pages, you'll find additional "what if's" with suggestions for variations to try. I hope these will help inspire you to experiment on your own.

Like many quilters, I have a special fondness for scrap quilts. Fan and circle blocks are perfect for scrap quilting. Each block presents a new opportunity to play with fabric combinations, bringing order out of the happy chaos of a good stash. All of the designs in the project section will work in scraps or planned color combinations, as well as in Stack-n-Whack® versions. Yardages and instructions for both versions are included. Whatever your choice of fabrics, techniques, and setting, I know you'll love the magic of making quilts by the slice!

part one:
general instructions

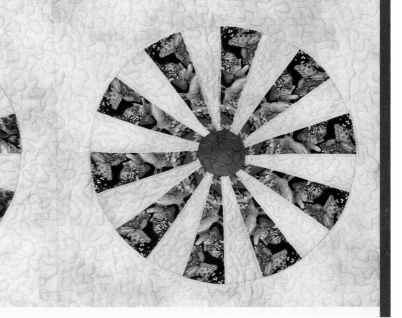

Fabric Selection Tips
Stack-n-Whack Wedges

Most medium- to large-scale prints will produce interesting Stack-n-Whack wedges. Small-scale prints can be effective if the wedges are also small. In general, choose a fabric with a repeat length that is longer than the wedge length you plan to use.

Look for prints with good contrast. Lively prints with a variety of shapes, lines, and colors make the most interesting blocks (Photo 1).

PHOTO 1. FLOURISHING FANS (detail). Look for contrast and variety within the print (quilt pattern and photo on page 48).

PHOTO 2. FANDANGO (detail), Sandy Curran, Newport News, Virginia. Bright prints and strong contrast create bold blocks (quilt photo on page 12).

PHOTO 3. SEA FANS (detail), Jo Ann Cooper, Spotsylvania, Virginia. Lower-contrast prints make softer blocks (quilt photo on page 13).

PHOTO 4. VERY VICTORIAN (detail). The mirror-image trick often creates a graceful swag design on fans (quilt pattern and photo on page 77).

Strong contrast or bright colors in the print will make bold kaleidoscope designs (Photo 2).

If you prefer a quieter look, choose a print with medium contrast (Photo 3).

Hand-printed fabrics, such as batiks, are not usually suitable for Stack-n-Whack. The design repeats are not as consistent as the repeats on commercial prints. These fabrics can be lovely in scrap fans, however.

Special effects are possible with certain types of prints. The magic mirror-image trick (Mirror-Image Piecing, on page 30) is especially effective in fan blocks. In this variation, the front and reverse sides of the fabric alternate from one wedge to the next. If the two sides are noticeably different, the fans may have a three-dimensional appearance (Photo 4).

Stripes and symmetrical prints can produce exciting designs if they are selectively cut (Photo 5).

To purchase the correct amount of yardage for a Stack-n-Whack fan project, you will need to know the length of the design repeat of the main fabric. For instructions on finding this measurement, read Finding and Cutting Layers, beginning on page 23.

Scrap or Strip-Cut Wedges

Your stash is your playground for scrap quilts. A variety of fabrics are featured in the project quilts (Photos 6, and 7 on page 14).

I hope you'll use these projects to showcase your own special collections. Setting a few guidelines can help you focus as you audition fabrics. For instance, RUNNING 'ROUND IN CIRCLES (project, page 110) features novelty prints. Because I used black and white prints for the background, I chose not to use any prints with white backgrounds in the wedges. I also selected prints

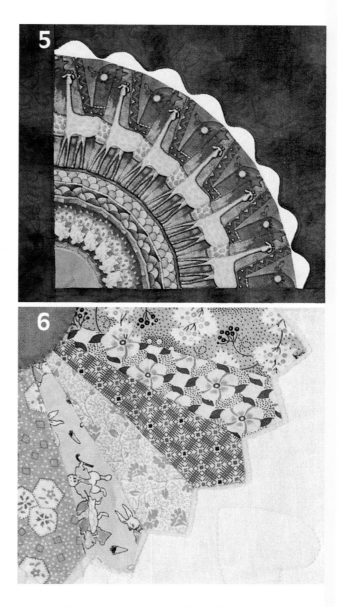

PHOTO 5. RAINBOWS & RICKRACK (detail). Stripes that run crosswise on the wedges create an arched effect (quilt pattern and photo on page 65).

PHOTO 6. SUGAR & SPICE (detail). Reproduction prints make great scrap quilts (quilt pattern and photo on page 88).

FANDANGO (58" x 66"), Sandy Curran, Newport News, Virginia. An exuberant tropical print and intense colors infuse this quilt with energy.

SEA FANS (53" x 72"), Jo Ann Cooper, Spotsylvania, Virgina. A soft main print and low contrast between the main fabric and background add to the tranquil feeling of this quilt.

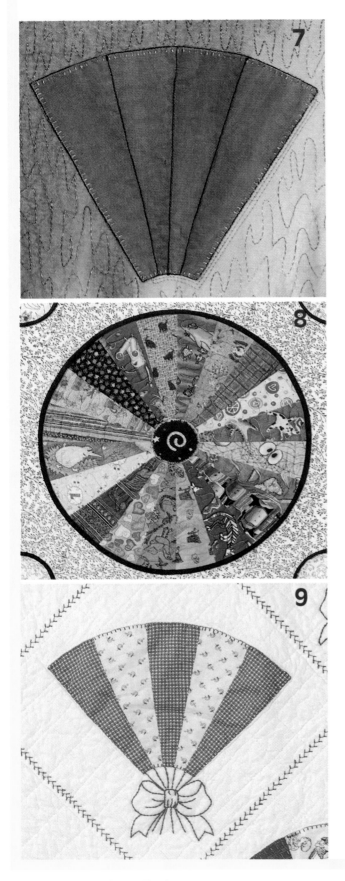

in color pairs as I placed them in each block, positioning the pairs opposite each other to give some balance and order to the design (Photo 8).

Background and Accent Fabrics

These fabrics should complement the fans or circles without competing with them for attention. Watch out for distracting background fabrics. If you suspect a print may be too busy when you look at the yardage, trust your judgment. Good choices for backgrounds include subtle, low-contrast fabrics with few colors, and monoprints or prints

PHOTO 7. FLOATING FANS (detail). Hand-dyed fabrics can be used (quilt pattern and photo on page 123).

PHOTO 8. RUNNING 'ROUND IN CIRCLES (detail). These prints are arranged in pairs based on color (quilt pattern and photo on page 110).

PHOTO 9. REDWORK RIBBONS (detail). White or cream backgrounds are especially appropriate with reproduction styles (quilt pattern and photo on page 58).

PHOTO 10. FANTASY FLORALS (detail), Dottie Lankard, Parsons, Kansas. When fans are set on a dark background, dark areas of the main print seem to disappear, creating a lacy effect (quilt photo, page 16)

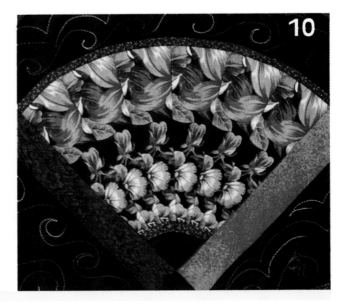

that appear as solids from a distance. Mottled textural prints are always a safe choice. Light solids are also traditional favorites (Photo 9).

Black or very dark backgrounds provide a dramatic setting for dark-ground prints (Photo 10).

Follow these same guidelines for the accent fabrics. If the accent fabric will be used as a bias edge trim or border, you can also consider stripes or other directional fabrics.

Supplies

The supplies you'll need for these projects are quite basic, and you may already have them on hand. If not, you'll find them readily available at most quilt shops or through mail-order quilt suppliers (see Sources, page 142).

Here are the essentials:

Rotary cutter. A 45-mm or larger blade is essential. If your blade is dull or nicked, treat yourself to a new one before you start. You will be able to cut faster, more accurately, and with much less effort. The extra-large 60-mm cutters make cutting multiple layers even easier.

Self-healing rotary cutting mat. Mats come in many configurations, but you'll want one that will allow you to cut across a folded width of fabric without having to shift the fabric. The minimum practical size for these projects is 17" x 23".

Rotary cutting rulers. Look for quality rulers with clearly marked ⅛" lines. A long rectangular ruler, 6" x 24", with 45° and 60° angle lines running in both directions, is especially versatile. A large, square ruler is handy for cutting the background fabric

Prewashing Recommendations

Prewashing can distort the fabric design, making it harder to match the repeats. This has been such a common problem for my students that I now advise against prewashing the main fabric for Stack-n-Whack projects. The multicolor prints commonly used for this method rarely bleed, but you can test a small swatch to be sure.

It is a good idea to prewash fabrics used for scrap quilts, as well as any background or accent fabrics that may bleed. Synthrapol® is a detergent additive available at many quilt shops (see Sources on page 142). A small amount added to the wash water will help prevent fugitive dyes from discoloring other fabrics. If you wash a finished quilt that contains many different fabrics, or if any of the fabrics have not been prewashed, this additive is good, inexpensive insurance.

If you prewash your fabric, try to make sure it dries evenly without twisting. Press carefully with the lengthwise grain before cutting, and use spray sizing to restore a crisp, smooth finish.

FANTASY FLORALS (47" x 60"), Dottie Lankard, Parsons, Kansas. A black background sets off a bright floral print. Colorful sashing and an unusual pieced border make this quilt distinctive.

squares (Figure 1–1). While templates are included for the wedges, special wedge rulers are convenient, accurate alternatives (see Sources, page 142).

Template-making materials. Fan bases, circle centers, and scalloped fan wedges are cut with templates. Make cutting templates from freezer paper or use copy paper and glue stick or basting spray (Figure 1–2). Some of the techniques also require pressing templates. These can be made from heat-resistant template material or lightweight cardboard, such as a recycled cereal box.

You may find these supplies helpful:

Flower-head pins. These are long pins with flat heads. They are useful for pinning stacks of fabrics, because they will not interfere with the ruler when you're cutting strips. If you do not have these, you can use pins with very small metal heads. But watch out because these are harder to see, and they may turn up under your cutting blade.

Spray sizing. For easier handling, spray your fabrics with sizing or light spray starch and press them dry before cutting your pieces. A bit of sizing during the final pressing will give blocks a crisp, neat finish, and it can do wonders for less-than-perfect piecing. Look for these products in the laundry aisle at a supermarket or chain store.

Seam roll. This sausage-shaped, tightly padded fabric tube allows you to press seam allowances open without catching the tip of your iron on nearby allowances. Look for one from a store or mailorder resource that sells dressmaking and tailoring notions. You can create a makeshift seam roll by tightly rolling a magazine and covering it with an old hand towel.

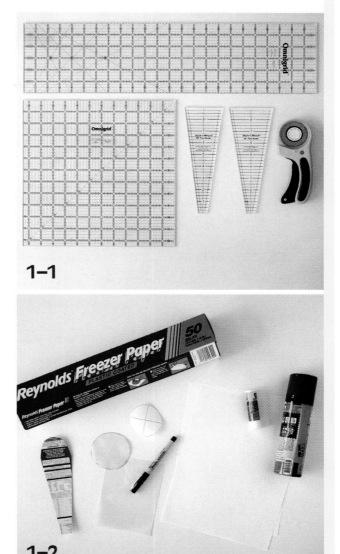

1–1

1–2

FIGURE 1–1. Rotary rulers and one type of cutter.

FIGURE 1–2. Supplies for making templates.

Bath towel. Place an old one over your ironing surface when pressing block units and finished blocks. The terry loops grip the fabric and help to prevent distortion.

Design wall. It is helpful to have a vertical surface on which you can place pieces or blocks to keep them in position until you're ready to sew them together. If you can place it where you can stand back from it a bit, the design wall will also help you decide on the overall arrangement of the blocks. A solid-colored sheet or an inexpensive fuzzy blanket makes a good design wall surface.

Using Templates

Several different types of templates will be needed for your projects: cutting templates for wedges and circles and pressing templates for creating smooth turned-under edges.

Wedge Cutting Templates

Trace the template on page 134 in the desired size on freezer paper. It's not necessary to trace the dotted seam allowance and center lines unless you plan to use the template for Stack-n-Select wedges (page 29).

Circle Templates

Because the circle patterns on page 133 are sized to use as pressing templates, they do not include seam allowances. For cutting fan bases with turned edges, use the size recommended in the instructions for your chosen quilt pattern and add a rough-cut ¼" seam allowance to the circle's edge. Straight-seam allowances are included in the sizes recommended for cutting quarter and half circles.

If you prefer, you can make your cutting templates with seam allowances. Simply

use a circle pattern one size (½") larger than the one called for in the pattern directions. Do not add seam allowances to full, quarter, or half circles that are to be fused in place. There are various finishes for raw-edge, fused appliqué (see page 31).

Refer to the pattern on page 133. When making a quarter- or half-circle template for cutting or pressing fabric pieces, mark the cutting lines on the template and use them as guides for cutting the circle apart, as follows:

For 90° fan bases, use the solid lines to cut the circle in quarters (Figure 1–3).

For 60° fan bases, use the dotted lines to cut the circle in sixths (Figure 1–4).

For 120° fan bases, use every other dotted line to cut the circle in thirds (Figure 1–5).

For half-circle bases, use the shaded area of the circle pattern. This area includes the seam allowance on the flat edge. Add a seam allowance to the curved edge only (Figure 1–6).

For projects using both quarter circles and half or full circles, the quarter-circle units should be one size (½") larger than the size used for the half or full circles.

Make a test circle before cutting all the fabric pieces. If you find that the size given does not cover the raw edge of the wedges adequately, try the next larger circle. Or, you may simply prefer the appearance of a larger fan base.

Making Pressing Templates

You can use lightweight cardboard or heat-resistant template material to make your pressing templates. Do not use a material that cannot withstand the heat of an iron at a medium setting.

To trace the circle pattern, use a hard pencil or a permanent marker that will not rub off on the fabric. If the template material used is transparent, you can trace the template directly from the pattern. For cardboard or other opaque materials, first trace the template shape on freezer paper or tracing paper. Iron the freezer paper to the cardboard or use glue stick to firmly attach the tracing paper to the cardboard. Cut the template carefully on the lines and check against the original shape for accuracy before using your template. Replace templates if they become worn or damaged. Purchased precut, circle pressing templates can also be used (see Sources, page 142).

Scalloped Wedge Pressing Templates

Use the template size that corresponds to the project wedge size. The template includes the seam allowance on the straight edges, but not on the curved edge. Align the straight edges of the template with the straight edges of the fabric wedges and press the allowance over the curved edge of the template.

Pointed Wedge Pressing Templates

This pressing template works for both 15° and 18° wedges in any size. Rotary cut a 2½" square from template material. Mark a diagonal line from corner to corner in both directions. Place any corner of the template into the folded pocket of the wedge. Align the pocket's seam line with the line on the template, then press.

Large Circle Templates

Use the following directions to make templates for circles that are larger than the patterns provided on page 133:

To make a large circle template for pressing under the edges of a full-circle fan, measure across the width of the pieced fan. Divide this measurement in half to find the

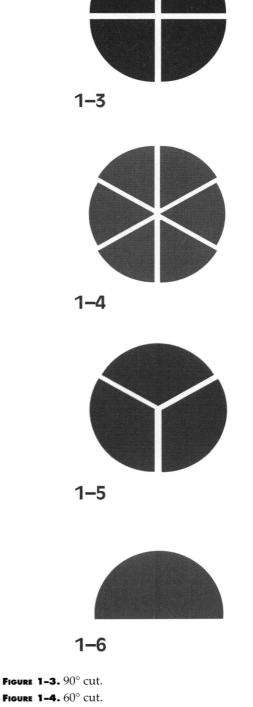

1–3

1–4

1–5

1–6

FIGURE 1–3. 90° cut.
FIGURE 1–4. 60° cut.
FIGURE 1–5. 120° cut.
FIGURE 1–6. Half-circle cut includes seam allowances on flat edge.

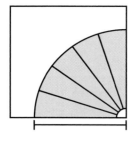

1–7

1–8

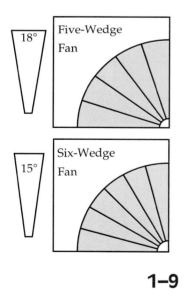

1–9

FIGURE 1–7. Measure from the block corner to the fan.

FIGURE 1–8. Comparing 15° and 18° wedges. Note that base is the same size for both.

FIGURE 1–9. Five 18° wedges make a 90° fan. Six 15° wedges make a 90° fan.

radius, then subtract ¼" for the seam allowance. Using a compass set to this measurement, draw a circle on your template material. Cut the template on the line.

For fans that are half circles, quarter circles, or other shapes, pin the pieced fan to a square of background fabric, aligning the sides of the fan with the edges of the square. Measure from the corner of the square to the raw outer edge of the fan (Figure 1–7). Subtract ¼" to find the radius to use for drawing the circle. Average the measurements for two or three fan blocks or use the smallest number for consistency.

If you plan to press under the inner edge of the fan instead of using a fan base, use a 1¼" radius for 15° wedges and a 1" radius for 18° wedges.

Cutting Wedges

Two different wedge shapes are used in the projects, a 15° and an 18° wedge. Both wedges are the same width at the base, but the 18° is wider at the outer edge (Figure 1–8).

You will need five 18° wedges or six 15° wedges to make a quarter fan (Figure 1–9).

For most projects, either wedge type may be used. However, it is important to follow the project cutting directions for the correct wedge type, because the number of pieces will vary. For Stack-n-Whack wedges, the stack must contain the right number of layers. The yardages will be slightly greater for 15° wedges, because an extra layer is needed for each stack.

Some designs work best with one type of wedge. For example, fans with two alternating colors, such as FRIENDSHIP FANS (photo page 82), look better with five 18° wedges. Fans made by using the mirror-image trick look more balanced with six 15° wedges (Figure 1–10).

Blocks based on 60° triangles or diamonds require 15° wedges (Figure 1–11).

Either wedge type can be used for circle designs (Figure 1–12).

These projects have wedges from 5" to 9" long. The width of the wedge at the outer edge determines the size of the fan or circle. As a rule, the wedge size given in the projects is 2" to 3" smaller than the block size. You can use a slightly smaller wedge if you would like more background fabric to show around the fan. In some cases, you can use a larger wedge. If you want to change the wedge or background block size, make a test block with the edge finishing techniques you plan to use (see Edge Finishes beginning on page 31), then check the proportions.

Wedges Cut from Strips

For wedges cut from strips, including those for Stack-n-Whack projects, see the directions and photos on page 23. For scrappieced designs, you can save time by cutting strips from each fabric to the required width and stacking several strips together to cut the wedges.

Individual Wedges

If you are cutting wedges from scraps that are too small to strip-cut, or if you want to selectively cut wedges (for example, from a novelty print), you can either make a template or purchase a special acrylic wedge ruler (see Sources, page 142).

FIGURE 1-10. Mirror-image fans. Compare the 18° fan on the top with the 15° fan on the bottom.

FIGURE 1-11. Use 15° wedges for triangle- and diamond-shapes.

FIGURE 1-12. You can use 15° or 18° wedges for circles.

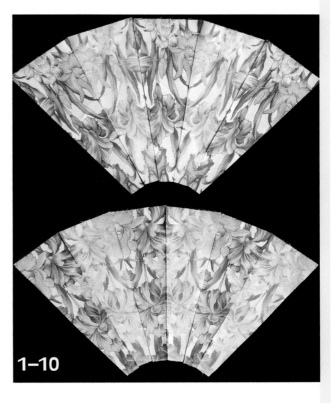

1–10

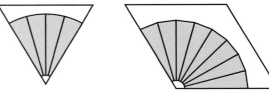

1–11

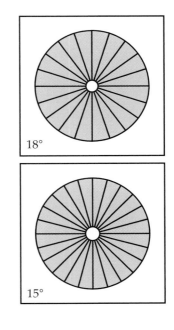

18°

15°

1–12

1–13

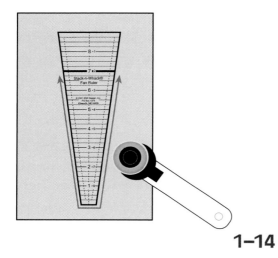

1–14

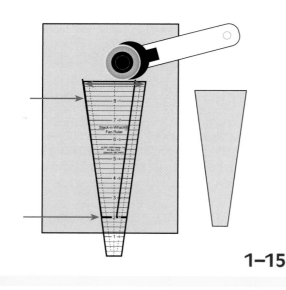

1–15

Wedge template:

1. Use the patterns on page 134 to make a paper, freezer-paper, or thin plastic template in the required size. Wedge patterns include seam allowances all around.

2. Place the template on the fabric and secure it with pins or a dab of glue stick (Figure 1–13). (Use an iron to press freezer-paper templates in place.)

3. Using an acrylic ruler as a straight edge to protect the template, rotary cut along all four sides of the wedge.

Wedge ruler:

1. Place the purchased ruler on the fabric and select the area you want to use.

2. Cut the narrow end of the wedge and the two long sides. Stop cutting just past the large number indicating the wedge size you want (Figure 1–14).

3. Keeping one edge of the ruler aligned with one long side of the wedge, slide the ruler down until the line with the small number indicating the wedge size is aligned with the narrow cut edge. Cut across the wide end of the wedge (Figure 1–15).

Symmetrical Wedges

When a fabric print contains symmetrical elements, you can produce blocks with mirror-image symmetry. To make symmetrical wedges, align the center line of the template or ruler along the center line of a motif, as shown in Figure 1–13. Cut the wedge as described in Individual Wedges

FIGURE 1–13. Secure template in place with a dab of glue stick.

FIGURE 1–14. Cut the narrow end and the long sides of the wedge first.

FIGURE 1–15. Slide the ruler down to the correct measurement to cut the top edge.

(page 21). When symmetrical wedges are sewn together, another mirror image will appear at the seam line. The number of different possible designs depends on the size of the template, the number of center lines in the print, and the distance between the center lines.

To get the most variety when cutting numerous sets, plan the placement for all the sets first. Mark around the ruler with chalk or other removable marker. Place the ruler on the marked lines again to cut each set.

Stack-n-Whack Wedges

This section outlines the procedure for preparing (stacking) and cutting (whacking) the fabrics to make sets of identical wedges (block kits). Each pieced block kit will have a unique design. While the number of layers to cut will vary depending on the design, the stacking process is the same for all projects. Each project includes a Stack-n-Whack chart. For instructions on using the chart, see How to Read a Stack-n-Whack Chart (page 136).

Finding and Cutting Layers

The repeats are cut from a single layer of fabric. In the projects, the stacks are cut from a half-width of fabric, which is generally 21"–22" wide.

To cut a half-width of fabric, begin by folding the fabric with selvages together to find the center. (If the fabric is wider than 45", measure 21" in from one selvage.) Cut or tear along the lengthwise grain (parallel to the selvages) for about a yard. Fold one half of the fabric out of the way and square off the cut end of the other half (Figure 1–16).

Figure 1–16. Square the 21"-wide end.

Figure 1–17. Measure the design repeat length.

Figure 1–18. Measuring two repeats.

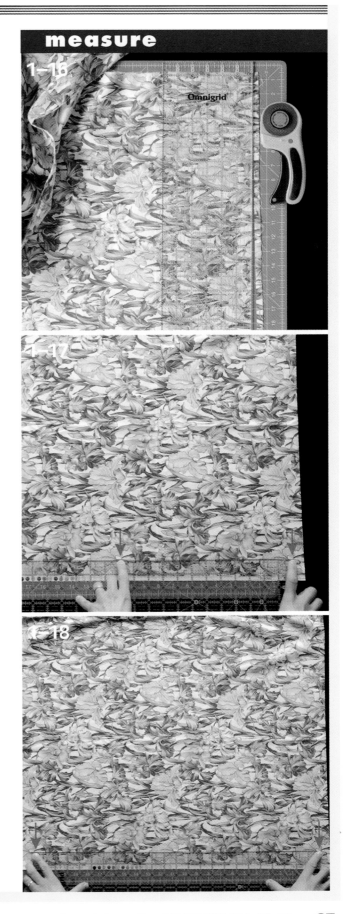

measure

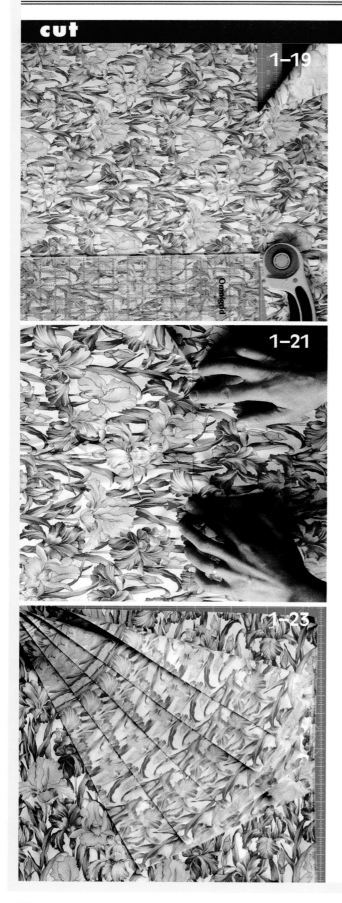

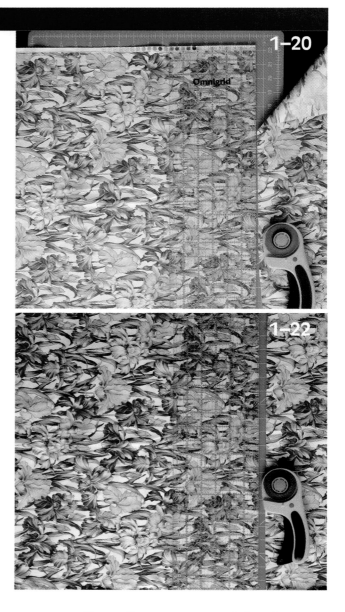

FIGURE 1-19. Use small rotary cuts to mark the selvage and the torn edge with the magic number.

FIGURE 1-20. Cut across the fabric, joining the two cut marks.

FIGURE 1-21. Use your fingers to align the design. The rectangle's edge will nearly disappear.

FIGURE 1-22. Cut the second layer along the matched edge.

FIGURE 1-23. Use the second piece to cut the remaining layers.

Switch the bulk of the fabric to your right if you are right-handed or to your left if you are left-handed. Smooth out the squared-off end of the fabric on your cutting mat.

The length of the layers to cut for the stack depends on the design repeat length of the print. To determine the repeat length, find a motif along one selvage. Glance along the selvage until you find the same motif in the same orientation. Measure between these two points to find the design repeat length. Check the Stack-n-Whack Chart (sample chart shown on page 137.) for your project to see how many repeats you will need for the layers and how many stacks to cut. The print in these photos has a repeat length of 11⅞" (Figure 1–17, page 23).

If the project instructions direct you to use just one repeat for each layer, you will use the length you have just measured for the length of the rectangle. If the instructions call for two or three repeats for each layer, count out that number of repeats and measure the total length. This length is the "magic number." It may be anywhere from 6" to 36", depending on the print and the project. This number will be the length of the rectangle. For the print shown, two repeats would measure 23¾" (Figure 1–18, page 23).

For the next step, ignore the print motifs. It no longer matters what part of the print you used as a reference to find the repeat length. Measure from the straightened edge along the selvage side to the magic number. Mark the length with a small cut from your rotary cutter. Measure and mark again at the torn side (Figure 1–19).

Align your ruler with the cut marks and cut across the width to make the first rectangle (Figure 1–20). With selvages and cut edges aligned, lay the first rectangle on the remaining fabric so that the print matches. Smooth out the rectangle and use your fingertips to match the design on the two layers all across the cut edge. The rectangle's edge should nearly disappear as it lines up with the print on the lower, uncut layer (Figure 1–21). The other end of the rectangle does not need to match up precisely.

When you have the top layer matched, lay your ruler down along the edge and cut across (Figure 1–22).

You now have two identical print rectangles. Set the top piece aside. Cut or tear along the length of the fabric, if necessary, and smooth out the portion you will be cutting. Use the second rectangle to cut a third layer and the remaining layers (Figure 1–23). The second rectangle will be the correct length, even if you have made a minor error in measuring or cutting the first rectangle. By using the second piece as a guide to cut the rest, you will not compound any errors. You will still be able to use the first layer in the stack, even if it is slightly shorter or longer than the rest. Repeat this process until you have the number of rectangular layers needed for the stack, as directed in the project instructions.

Be sure to cut all these layers from the same half of the fabric. Printing and finishing processes can cause slight distortions even in high quality fabrics, and the differences may be noticeable in the finished blocks if you use crosswise, rather than lengthwise, repeats. You may also find that the crosswise repeats are staggered, so that they only match up for part of the width. This can result in a stack that is too narrow to cut enough block kits for the project.

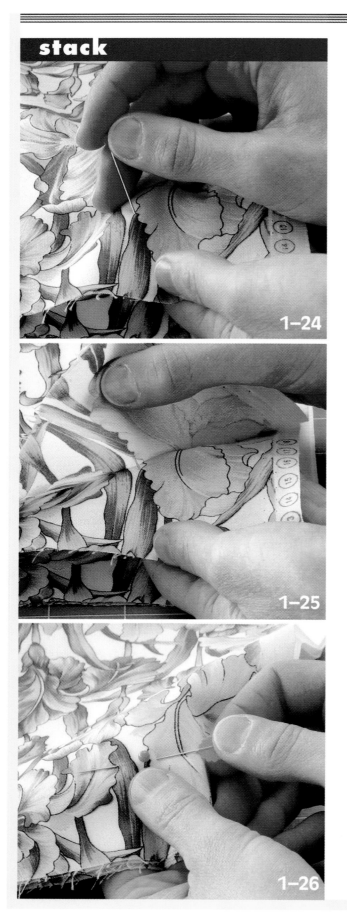

1–24

1–25

1–26

Stacking the Layers

Press the layers one at a time to remove any wrinkles. Press along the lengthwise grain to avoid distortion. If you have pre-washed the fabric, it is a good idea to use a little sizing or spray starch to return some crispness to the fabric. Starch will make the pieces easier to handle and will help keep the edges from stretching.

Stack the layers and smooth out each piece so that the selvages align. When you have all the layers stacked, use the following stick-pinning method to align the motifs accurately through the layers. You'll need

FIGURE 1–24. Place the pin on a distinctive part of the design.

FIGURE 1–25. Put the pin through the same spot on all the layers.

FIGURE 1–26. Hold the stick pin and fabric layers tight. Push a flower-head pin through all the layers.

FIGURE 1–27. Pin along the cut edge and both sides.

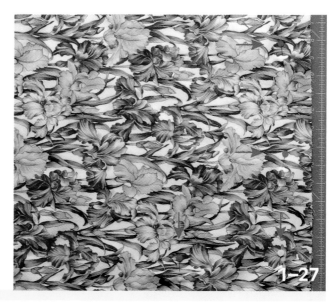

1–27

one pin with a large round head, and several flower-head pins. These are long pins with a large flat head that will not interfere with the ruler. If you do not have these, you can use long pins with small metal heads. These are harder to see, though, so take extra care to keep stray pins out of the way of your cutting blade.

To stick-pin fabric layers, select a point on the fabric design about 1"–1½" from the crosswise (cut) edge. Look for something that's easy to spot, such as the tip of a leaf. Place the point of the round-headed pin on this spot (Figure 1–24).

Lift the top layer of fabric and slide the pin through. Find the same point on the next layer and slide the pin through it. Continue lifting layers and pinning through this point in the design until you have gone through all the layers (Figure 1–25).

Slide the pin all the way through to the head and hold it in place with your thumb and forefinger. Hold the pin straight up and down and smooth out the surrounding fabric. Use a flower-head pin to pin through all the layers, right beside the stick pin (Figure 1–26).

Remove the stick pin. Lay the fabric down flat and repeat the pinning process at three other points across the width. For additional accuracy, also pin along the selvage and torn edge (Figure 1–27).

Whacking Wedge Block Kits

Be sure to use the correct wedge type. For 4, 6, 8, and 12 layer stacks, use the 15° wedge. For 5 and 10 layer stacks, use the 18° wedge. The wedge patterns on page 134 include ¼" seam allowances.

The strip cutting method shown produces random, unplanned kaleidoscopic effects. To selectively cut the block kits, see the Stack-n-Select instructions on page 29.

Trim the stack along the pinned crosswise edge to ensure a straight edge through all the layers (Figure 1–28, page 28).

Turn the stack around or rotate the mat. Cut a strip through all the layers, using the strip width measurement given in the directions for your project. To cut strips wider than your ruler, measure along the top edge of the stack and mark the strip width with a small cut from your rotary cutter. Repeat for the bottom edge of the stack (Figure 1–29, page 28).

Cut the strip into wedges, removing pins as you go to protect the rotary cutter blade: Place the template or wedge ruler at one end of the strip set, aligning the narrow end of the template or ruler with one edge of the strip and the wide end of the template (or the ruler's line for the wedge size) with the other edge of the strip. If you are using a paper or thin plastic template, use a ruler as a straightedge to protect the template. Cut one long side of the first wedge (Figure 1–30, page 28).

Rotate the strip set so the just-cut edge is toward you. Cut the other side of the wedge (Figure 1–31, page 28).

For each new cut, rotate the template or ruler a half-turn and align the narrow end with the strip edge and one long side with the just-cut angled edge. Cut wedges as needed, rotating the ruler for each cut.

For more accurate cutting, repin the crosswise edge before cutting each additional strip.

Making Additional Stacks

If the project requires a second stack, cut the stack from the remaining width of the fabric, starting with a new first layer. This stack should produce a new assortment of

1-28

Figure 1-28. Trim the stack along the pinned edge.

Figure 1-29a and b. How to cut a strip wider than your ruler. The strip shown is 8" wide.

Figure 1-30. Use a template or wedge ruler to cut wedges (wedge ruler shown).

Figure 1-31. Turn the fabric and cut the other side.

1-29a

1-29b

1-30

1-31

blocks. If the crosswise repeats line up side by side with the first stack, trim an inch or two from the beginning edge of the fabric to offset the pattern before cutting the first layer. Off-setting the cut will ensure that these kits will be different from your previous ones.

Stack-n-Select Wedges

Use this method to selectively cut wedge kits, for example from novelty prints or symmetrical prints. Fabrics are stacked as you would for Stack-n-Whack, but instead of cutting wedges from strips, cut individual kits, using paper templates, as described on page 22. To aid in placement, make a window template. Trace the desired wedge size and shape on paper or template material. Draw ¼" seam allowances inside the template shape (templates include seam allowances). Cut out the interior of the template on the seam line to create a window. After selecting an area to use, place the paper template under the window template. Hold in place with glue stick or pins. Remove the window template and cut around the wedge, using a straight edge.

Joining Wedges

Use the following instructions to join your wedges. For mirror-image wedges, see Mirror-Image Piecing on page 30.

Basic Wedge Piecing

For Stack-n-Whack kits, use a set of identical wedges for each block. For other blocks, such as those made from scraps, arrange the wedges for each block as desired before piecing.

Sew the wedges together in pairs, right sides together, matching the top and bottom edges. For five-wedge fans, use four of the wedges to make two pairs, but be sure to keep the fifth wedge with the set. Do not press the seam allowances yet (Figure 1–32).

Join the pairs, flipping the previous seam allowances away from the needle so

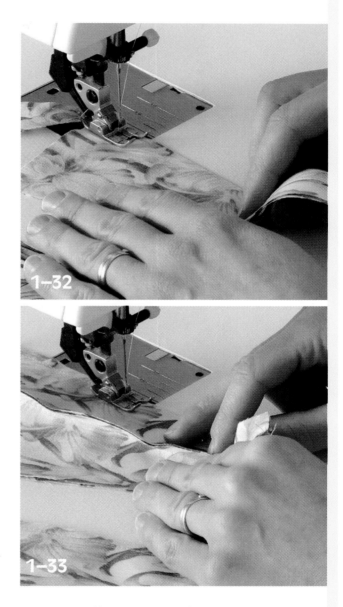

FIGURE 1-32. Chain-sew the wedges into pairs.

FIGURE 1-33. Then sew the pairs together.

1–34

1–35

1–36

they will not get caught in the seam. For five-wedge fans, sew two pairs together, then add the fifth wedge to complete the fan (Figure 1–33, page 29).

Use the tip of your iron to press the seam allowances open. Press them from the outer edge toward the center of the fan (Figure 1–34).

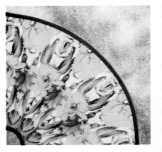

Mirror-Image Piecing

This Stack-n-Whack variation is pieced the same way as the basic fan, with one difference. Instead of sewing the wedges right sides together, sew each pair of wedges just as they are stacked. The wrong

FIGURE 1–34. Press seam allowances open.

FIGURE 1–35. Both wedges are right side up.

FIGURE 1–36. Every other wedge in the fan will be wrong side up.

FIGURE 1–37. Fold the wedges in half and use chain piecing to sew across the top of each one.

1–37

side of one wedge will face the right side of the other (Figure 1–35).

Sew the pairs together. Adjust the edges so that the printed design matches as closely as possible at the seam lines (Figure 1–36).

Edge Finishes

The edges of your fans can be finished in various ways before they are appliquéd to the background. If you prefer, your fans can be fused to the background and the raw edges top-stitched or covered with decorative trim (page 39).

Pointed Wedges

Fold each wedge in half lengthwise, right sides together, so that the top corners meet. Stitch across the wide end from the raw edges to the fold. Chain piece the wedges for quicker piecing. For Stack-n-Whack wedges, clip the block kits apart, leaving the matching wedges chained together until ready for the next step (Figure 1–37).

Clip the folded corner of each wedge at an angle to reduce the bulk. Turn the point right side out (Figure 1–38, page 32).

Using the tip of a seam ripper or other pointed tool, work the corner out to a neat point (Figure 1–39, page 32).

Troubleshooting

▌ Make sure the wedges are cut accurately. If you place two wedges right sides together, they should match at each corner. Discard inaccurately cut wedges or cut them a smaller size for another project.

▌ If the fan bows out at the inner or outer edges, or will not lie flat, check to see that all seam allowances are a consistent ¼" and adjust if necessary.

▌ Pulling on the wedges while piecing or pressing can distort the fabric. To repair distortion, place the fan on an ironing surface covered with a towel and use a steam iron to block the fan into shape.

▌ If your fan seems skewed to one side, the sewing machine feed system may be at fault. To compensate for this problem, try sewing the seams in alternate directions. For example, when sewing the wedges into pairs, sew from the narrow end to the wide end. When joining the pairs, sew from the wide end to the narrow end.

▌ Fans can become distorted if you add each wedge individually instead of making the pairs first, then joining the pairs.

Skewed fan.

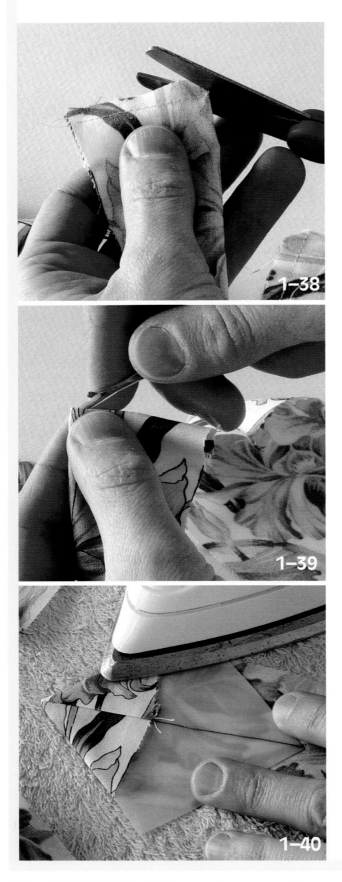

To press the points, use a square pressing template (Making Pressing Templates, page 19) marked with diagonal lines from corner to corner. Slip the template into the pocket formed at the tip of the wedge. Make sure the center line on the template aligns with the center fold line of the wedge and the seam line on the point. Press the turned edges only (Figure 1–40). Slip the template out and press again. Flip the wedge over and press the edges from the right side.

To sew the wedges together, match the folded edges at the top and the raw edges at the bottom (Figure 1–41). Continue piecing as for the basic fan.

For mirror-image pointed wedges, fold and stitch half the wedges, from each block kit, right side out and half wrong side out. When sewing them together, alternate the wedges so that every other one will be wrong side out.

Figure 1–38. Clip the corners.

Figure 1–39. Push the corners out.

Figure 1–40. Press the points with a pressing template.

Figure 1–41. To join wedges, align the top and bottom edges.

Scalloped Wedges

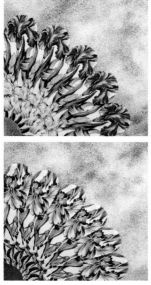

Cut the fabric wedges as usual. Make a scalloped wedge pressing template of the required size from the patterns on page 135. Place the top edge of the scalloped template ¼" from the top of the wedge. Trim the fabric corners ¼" from the curved edge of the template (Figure 1–42).

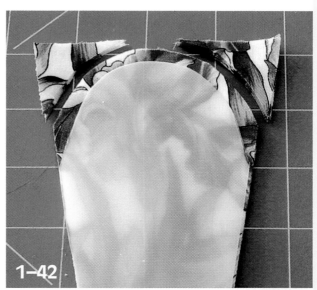

The curved edge can be gathered and turned to the back of the wedge, as follows: Baste each wedge ⅛" from the curved edge (Figure 1–43). If you are chain sewing the basting stitches, leave at least 2" of thread between the wedges. When cutting the wedges apart, leave a long enough tail on each one for gathering the edge.

Place the scallop template on the back of the wedge, with the side edges aligned and the top of the template ¼" from the top edge of the wedge. Draw the seam allowance to the back by pulling gently on one thread tail at each end. Distribute the fullness evenly and press the edge over the template (Figure 1–44).

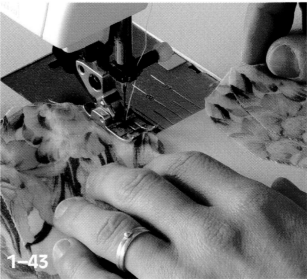

Slide out the pressing template and press again. A bit of spray sizing will help to hold the seam allowance in place.

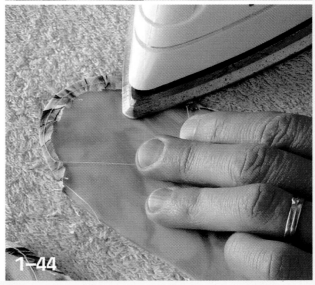

Figure 1–42. Trim scalloped wedges ¼" from the template.

Figure 1–43. Baste ⅛" from the curved edge.

Figure 1–44. Gather the allowance in back of the wedge and press over the template.

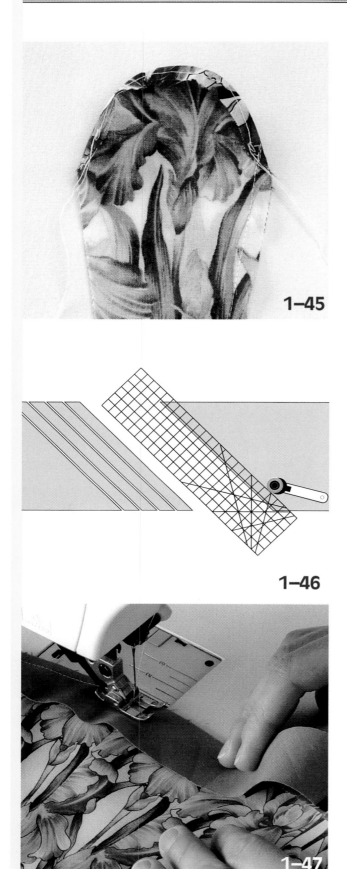

1–45

1–46

1–47

To piece a block, sew the wedges together, matching the folded edges at the top and the raw edges at the bottom (Figure 1–45). Continue piecing as for the basic fan.

For mirror-image scalloped wedges, draw the seam allowance to the right side for half the wedges and to the wrong side for the other half. Alternate the right side and wrong side wedges when piecing them together.

Bias-Strip Edge

Cut a strip across the width of the accent fabric, 3" wider than the wedge size. As an example, for 8" wedges, cut an 11" strip. Unfold the strip. Using the 45° line of the ruler on one long edge, cut bias strips 1¼" wide from the strip (Figure 1–46).

You will need one bias strip for each outer fan edge, and one-third of a strip for each inner edge. For the edges of full circles, cut a wider strip of accent fabric, or piece the bias strips to create the length needed.

With right sides together and raw edges matching, sew a bias strip to the outer edge of the fan with a ¼" seam allowance. Be careful not to stretch the bias strip (Figure 1–47).

Press the strip away from the fan (Figure 1–48). Turn the fan over and press the strip down over the seam allowance (Figure 1–49).

Figure 1–45. To join wedges, align top and bottom edges.

Figure 1–46. Cut bias 1¼" strips.

Figure 1–47. Sew the bias strip to the fan edge.

Press again from the right side. Trim the bias strip even with the edges of the fan.

Follow the same steps to apply the bias trim to the inner edge. Carefully adjust the lower edges of the wedges so that they align with the strip. Stitch with the wrong side of the fan facing up to allow more control. To help prevent the inner edge from stretching, gently ease the wedges toward the presser foot as you sew (Figure 1–50).

For circles, leave one seam open between two of the wedges, and apply the bias strip. Press the strip over the seam allowance. Sew the remaining wedge seam, continuing the stitching through the bias strip (Figure 1–51).

Fold the strip over to the back and press in place (Figure 1–52, page 36).

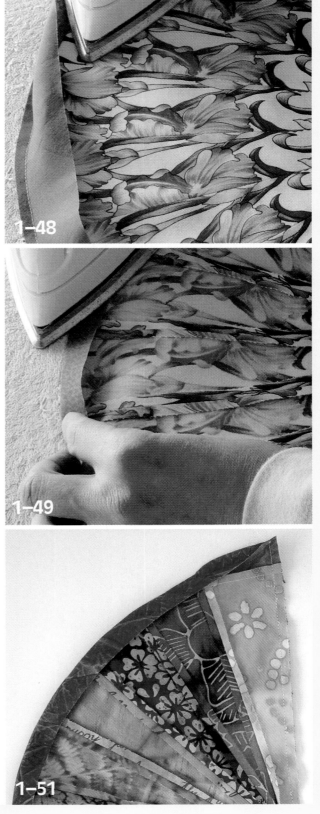

1–48

1–49

Figure 1–48. Press the bias strip up.

Figure 1–49. Press the bias strip down over the edge.

Figure 1–50. Ease the wedges toward the presser foot.

Figure 1–51. Sew the last wedge seam after sewing the bias strip to the edge of the circle.

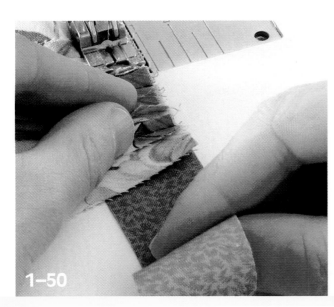

1–50

1–51

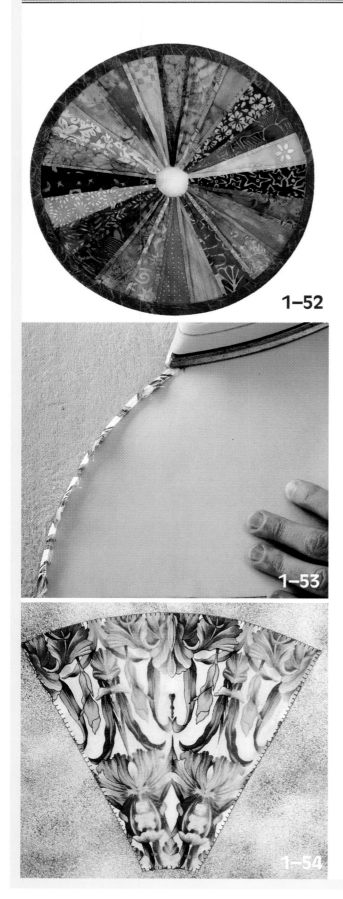

1–52

Pressed-Under Edge

Stitch ⅛" from the outer edge of the fan. Pull gently on the threads to ease in the fullness. Press ¼" of the edge to the back of the fan. For a smooth finish, use a pressing template (Figure 1–53). See page 18 for information on making pressing templates for fans.

All four edges can be pressed under before appliquéing the fan to the background (Figure 1–54).

To turn under the inner curved edge of a fan, stitch ⅛" from the edge. Pull out a few stitches in the seam allowances between the wedges, so that the curved seam allowance will lie flat. Turn ¼" of the edge to the back of the fan and press.

Appliquéing Wedges

Press the fan carefully so that it will lie smoothly on the background square. Place the fan on the square so that the outer corners touch the edges of the block. For more accurate placement, you can measure the background from the corner of the block to the corner of the fan on each side and adjust the placement so that the measurements are equal (Figure 1–55).

FIGURE 1–52. Fold the bias strip to the back.

FIGURE 1–53. Use a pressing template (page 18) for a smooth edge.

FIGURE 1–54. Turned edges with blanket stitch.

Pin the fan in place at the outer and inner edges. If the wedges extend beyond the edges of the background square at the inside corner, check the troubleshooting tips on page 31. This problem is common when the bias finish is used at the lower edge. If the distortion is minor, you can trim the wedges even with the edges of the background square after stitching the fan in place (Figure 1–56).

For full circles, fold the background square in quarters and press lightly. Unfold the square and use the creases to center the pieced circle on the background. Match the seam lines or the center lines of the wedges to the creases.

For 60° or 120° fans, align the edges of the fan with two adjacent edges of the background triangle or diamond (Figure 1–57).

FIGURE 1–55. Place the fan by measuring the background from the corners to the fan.

FIGURE 1–56. Trim away minor distortions.

FIGURE 1–57a AND b. Fan placement for triangles and diamonds.

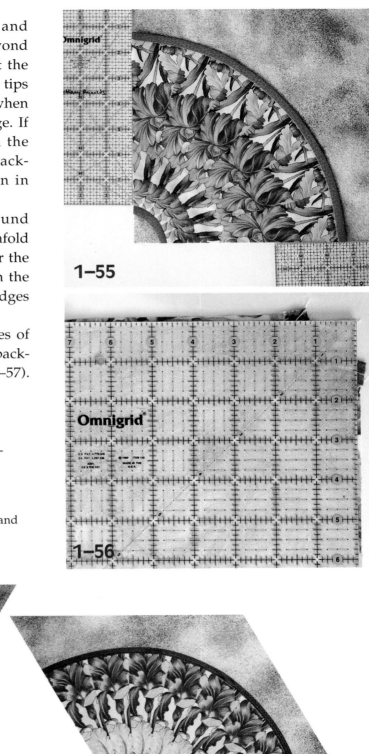

1–55

1–56

1–57a

1–57b

1-58

1-59

Measure the background from the corner of the block to the corner of the fan on each side and adjust so that the measurements are the same.

Fans finished with the bias-edge technique can be attached to the background fabric by stitching in the ditch between the wedges and the bias trim. For inconspicuous stitching, sew with the needle in the wedges, right next to the bias strip (Figure 1–58).

The bias trim can be left as a dimensional accent or stitched down close to the outer edge with a machine or hand appliqué stitch (Figure 1–59).

Blind Stitch

Appliqué the fans in place with a blind stitch, by hand or machine. Use a thread color that blends with the fabric. If you are not familiar with the machine blind stitch, check your machine's manual. If the width

FIGURE 1–58. Sew close to the bias strip.

FIGURE 1–59. The bias strip can be sewn along the outer edge.

FIGURE 1–60a AND b. Machine blind-hem stitched fan edges.

1-60a

1-60b

and length settings are adjustable, vary the settings until you find one you like, then make a note of it. Use a presser foot that offers good visibility, such as an open-toed appliqué foot. When stitching, keep the straight portion of the stitch on the background fabric. When the needle swings over for the zigzag portion of the stitch, it should catch the edge of the fan (Figure 1–60).

Blanket Stitch

If you have the blanket stitch on your machine, it is a quick and attractive option for attaching the fans. You can make this finish inconspicuous by using a narrow stitch width and matching thread, or you can accent the edge with a decorative thread and a wider stitch setting (Figure 1–61).

Decorative Trims

Fused Bias-Edge

Fusible folded-edge bias trims are available in a number of colors, or you can make your own by using a bias-making tool and narrow precut fusible web.

Attach the fan to the background fabric by stitching a scant ⅛" from the curved edges. Follow the manufacturer's instructions to fuse the bias trim to the fan so it covers the edge and the stitching line (Figure 1–62).

Use a straight stitch, blind hem stitch, or blanket stitch to sew the bias trim close to both edges (Figure 1–63, page 40). For circles, turn under the raw ends of the bias trim so they meet.

Alternatively, you can make raw-edge bias trim, as follows:

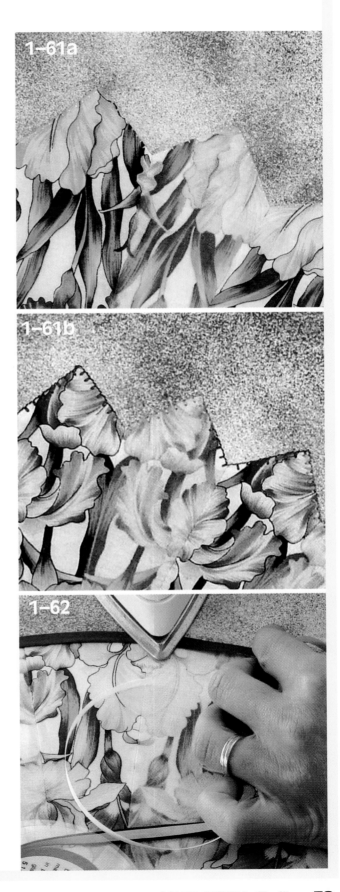

Figure 1–61a and b. Machine blanket stitched edges.

Figure 1–62. Fused bias trim.

Fuse a rectangle of webbing to the reverse side of the accent fabric. Rotary cut the accent fabric in ¼" or ⅜" bias strips. Fuse the bias trim to the fan so that it covers the edge and the stitching line. Use a blanket stitch or zigzag stitch to secure the raw edges of the trim.

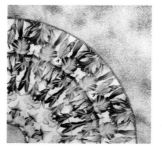

Cording

Couched cording adds definition to the fan edges. Consider narrow twisted cording, embroidery floss, pearl cotton, or any narrow, flexible trim. Use the pressed-under edge or the pointed or scalloped wedges. Attach the fan first with a blind stitch. Lay the cording next to the edge of the fan as you sew it in place with a zigzag stitch in a matching or contrasting color (Figure 1–64).

For circles, draw the ends of the cording through to the back of the block and secure. If the cording is too heavy to draw to the back, secure the ends with a seam sealer or a bit of fabric glue to prevent raveling.

Rickrack and Lace

Wide rickrack trim adds a fun touch to the fan edge. To apply the rickrack, work with the back of the fan facing

FIGURE 1–63. Straight-stitched bias trim.

FIGURE 1–64. Add cording for definition.

FIGURE 1–65. Sew rickrack trim ¼" from the edge.

upward and the rickrack underneath. Position the rickrack so that the raw edge of the fan touches the "valleys" in the rickrack. Stitch ¼" from the edge of the fan (Figure 1–65).

Trim the rickrack even with the fan edge and press the seam allowances over to the back (Figure 1–66).

Stitch the fan in place by sewing the rickrack close to the seam line. If desired, stitch close to the curved edge of the rickrack as well (Figure 1–67).

Lace may be added to a finished edge as an embellishment (Photo 1–11). Lace trims may also be used to finish an edge. Sew the trim to the right side of the fan, press the edges to the back, and stitch in the seam line.

Adding Fan Bases

Many of the projects shown have bases cut from whole, quarter, or half circles. Here are two methods for preparing these.

Folded-Edge Method

Use the template size recommended in the project directions or a larger size if you prefer. Trace the template on freezer paper. Include the cutting lines for quarter- or half-circles. Cut out the circle and place the shiny side of the freezer paper on the reverse side of the base fabric. Press to temporarily adhere the circle to the fabric. Using a long stitch length, stitch around the paper, ⅛" outside the edge (Figure 1–68, page 43).

FIGURE 1–66. Press the seam allowances toward the fan.

FIGURE 1–67. Close-up of wide rickrack.

PHOTO 11. ROSE ARRIVES AT THE BLACK & WHITE BALL (detail). Jo Ann Cooper, Spotsylvania, Virginia. Lace adds an extra flourish to the center fan (quilt photo on page 42).

ROSE ARRIVES AT THE BLACK & WHITE BALL (47" x 64"), Jo Ann Cooper, Spotsylvania, Virginia. A single fan cut from a black rose print takes center stage.

Cut the circle from the base fabric, leaving a ¼" seam allowance around the paper circle. Take care not to clip the thread tails (Figure 1–69).

Pull gently on a thread tail at each end to draw the seam allowance over to the back. Insert a pressing template cut from heat-resistant template material or card stock (page 18). The pressing template should line up with the freezer paper circle (Figure 1–70).

Distribute the gathers evenly around the edge of the circle and press (Figure 1–71).

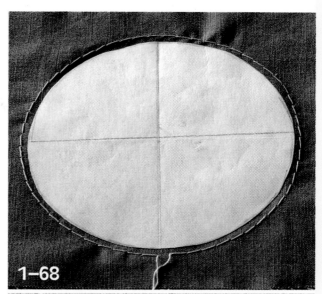

FIGURE 1–68. Stitch around the paper ⅛" outside the edge.

FIGURE 1–69. Cut the fabric circle with a ¼" seam allowance.

FIGURE 1–70. Place a pressing template inside the circle.

FIGURE 1–71. Press the edge of the circle.

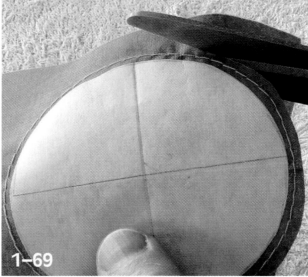

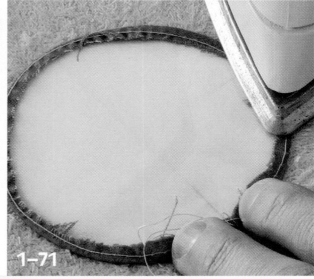

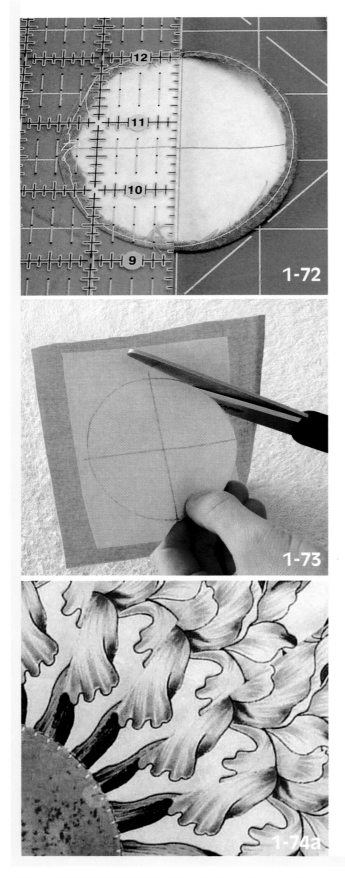

1-72

Remove the pressing template and press the circle again. Use sizing or starch to help secure the edge. For quarter-circles, 60° wedges, or 120° wedges, cut the circle apart on the cutting lines (Figure 1–72). For half-circles, cut ¼" beyond the center line to add a seam allowance to the straight edge. Use only the larger section. Remove the freezer paper.

Raw-Edge Method

Use the template size recommended in the project directions or a larger size if you prefer. Trace the template on the paper side of a paper-backed fusing web. Include the cutting lines for quarter- or half-circles. Cut out the circle and place the web on the reverse side of the base fabric. Press in place, following the fusible web manufacturer's directions. Cut out the circle on the marked line (Figure 1–73).

FIGURE 1–72. Cut on the lines to make half and quarter circles.

FIGURE 1–73. Cut the circle on the line.

FIGURE 1–74. Raw-edge finishes. (a) Buttonhole stitch. (b) Zigzag.

1-73

1-74a

1-74b

Appliquéing Fan Bases

Pin the fan base in place on the block, covering the raw edges at the narrow end of the wedges. For whole circles, crease the accent circle in quarters to aid in centering it on the wedge circle. Use your preferred method to appliqué the bases in place (Figure 1–74).

Trimming Background Fabric

Trimming is optional, but recommended, because it will make the top easier to hand or machine quilt. To trim, turn the fan block over and cut ¼" from the stitching line at the inner and outer curved edges (Figure 1–75).

If you have turned under the edges of the fan base, you can also trim away the fabric under the base. For pointed wedges, you may want to trim away the extra fabric behind the points to keep the seam or the print from showing on the right side (Figure 1–76).

Quilting Suggestions

Whether you plan to hand or machine quilt your project, you'll want to give some thought to a quilting design that will complement and enhance your top. Because the fans are clearly the focal point of these quilts, you can emphasize them with outline quilting. With care, this step can be done in free-motion. Before doing the free-motion quilting, however, it's best to do all the machine-guided straight-line quilting first. Anchor borders and sashing with straight-line quilting for stability and crisp definition. This quilting can be hidden in the seam line or stitched ⅛"– ¼" away from the seam.

Blocks that are separated by contrasting sashing may not need additional background quilting, especially if they are small. Larger blocks will benefit from some simple filler quilting, such as stippling.

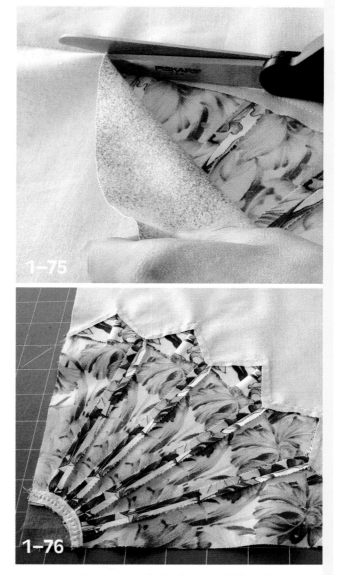

Figure 1–75. Trim away the background fabric from behind the fan.

Figure 1–76. You can also trim the fabric behind the wedge points.

When the blocks are set side by side, on point, or with a sashing in the same fabric as the block background, there may be more background area to fill. If you prefer to avoid marking, stipple quilting and other free-motion filler patterns can be used. Geometric designs, such as the grid quilting used for REDWORK RIBBONS (page 58) can be effective too. Sizing a motif to fit the background area is also an option, such as the heart design in SUGAR & SPICE (page 88). Quilting motifs designed to fit in half-square triangles may be adaptable to the background area in the corners of the blocks. If you are game to try your own design, look to your main fabric for inspiration for quilting motifs.

The fans or circles themselves can be quilted in numerous ways. For a simple machine-guided approach, stitch along the seam lines between the wedges to define them and add dimension. Try using a narrow zigzag stitch in a decorative thread. Because the zigzag stitch straddles the seam line, it is less likely to cut the piecing thread in the pressed-open seams. FRAMED FANS (page 72) shows this quilting option. You can also quilt two or more arcs across each fan, following the natural curve of the fan as in FLOURISHING FANS (page 48).

Stack-n-Whack blocks are often enhanced with free-motion quilting that follows the unique motif in each block. Just choose a few lines in the fabric to emphasize and follow the same lines as you quilt from wedge to wedge. The KYOTO FANS blocks are quilted in this style (page 12).

part two:
quilt
patterns

Flourishing Fans

Flourishing Fans

Finished Block Size: 10"
Finished Quilt Top: 60½" x 74½"
Wedge Length: 8"
Wedge Type Shown: 18° (5 per fan)

T he simple on-point setting has always been a favorite for fan blocks. Setting triangles, in a slightly darker value, frame these five-wedge, pointed fans. To use this setting with a different block size, use the On-Point Setting reference chart on page 138.

Fabric Requirements
Measurements in yards unless otherwise indicated.

If the design repeat of **Main Fabric** is	6"–10"	11"–14"	15"–17"	18"–26"	over 26"
You will need this many yards for the Stack-n-Whack version: with 18°, 5-wedge fans (as shown)	4⅝	4⅜	5¼	4	5 repeats
with 15°, 6-wedge fans	5½	5⅛	6¼	4⅞	6 repeats
Or, for strip-cut or scrap fan wedges	2½ yds. or equivalent in scraps				

Additional Fabrics	
Background Fabric	2⅝
Fan Accent Fabric (fan base)	¼
Border Setting Fabric	1⅝
Backing (pieced crosswise)	3¾
Binding (cut 2½" strips crosswise)	⅝

Cutting Stack-n-Whack Wedges

Prepare the main fabric, following the directions on pages 23–29.

Stack-n-Whack Chart for Flourishing Fans
Cut layers 21" wide. Cut 5 identical layers for 18° fans, or 6 identical layers for 15° fans.
Use a different set of identical repeats for each additional stack.

If the lengthwise design repeat is:	Use this many design repeats:	Make this many stacks:
6" – 10"	Three repeats per layer	2
11" – 18"	Two repeats per layer	2
Over 18"	One repeat per layer	2

Whack...	To make...
(4) 8" strips across width	(32) wedge block kits (8–9 per strip)

Cutting Strip-Cut or Scrap Wedges

Cut 8" wedges, following the instructions starting on page 20. You will need (160) 18° wedges for 5-wedge fans, or (192) 15° wedges for 6-wedge fans.

Cutting Background and Border Setting Fabrics		
Fabric	**First Cut**	**Second Cut**
Background	(8) 10½" strips across width	(32) 10½" squares (4 per strip)
Border Setting	(2) 15½" strips across width	(4) 15½" squares. Cut each square twice on the diagonal to make (14) side triangles, plus 2 extras.
Border Setting	(2) 8" squares from remainder of the 15½" strips	Cut each square once on the diagonal to make (4) corner triangles.
Border Setting	(8) 2½" strips across the width. Piece together to make one long strip.	

Making the Blocks

Piece 32 fans, using your choice of techniques. The sample quilt has pointed wedges (page 31) and appliqued quarter-circle bases (page 41). Appliqué the fans to the background squares.

For the fan bases, prepare (8) 3" circles (pattern on page 133) and cut to make 32 quarter-circles. Appliqué the bases to the fan blocks.

Assembling the Quilt Top

Arrange the fan blocks and setting triangles, following the quilt assembly diagram, Figure 2–1, page 52. Sew the seams in each diagonal row, then sew the diagonal rows together.

Measure the quilt top down the center and cut two pieces to this length from the pieced 2½" strip of border setting fabric. Sew the strips to the two long sides.

Measure across the width in the center of the quilt. Cut two strips of border setting fabric to this length. Sew the strips to the top and bottom.

What if...

I'd like to add a border to make this quilt a little larger?

To add a simple unpieced border, cut an additional 2½ yds. of fabric in four lengthwise strips of the desired width. Borders cut 10" wide will increase the finished size to 79½" x 93½".

FIGURE 2-1. Quilt top assembly.

Flip-Flop Fans

Flip-Flop Fans

Finished Block Size: 12"

Finished Quilt Top: 49" x 73"

Wedge Length: 9"

Wedge Type Shown: 15° (6 per fan)

I n this arrangement, the fans are "flip-flopped" in alternating rows. This setting adapts easily to adding or subtracting rows of blocks.

Fabric Requirements
Measurements in yards unless otherwise indicated.

If the design repeat of **Main Fabric** is	6"–10"	11"–14"	15"–17"	18"–26"	over 26"
You will need this many yards for the Stack-n-Whack version: with 18°, 5-wedge fans	3⅛	2¼	2⅝	4	5 repeats
with 15°, 6-wedge fans (as shown)*	3¾	2⅝	3⅛	4⅞	6 repeats
Or, for strip-cut or scrap fan wedges	1⅝ yds. or equivalent in scraps				

Additional Fabrics	
Background Fabric	3⅛
Fan Accent Fabric (single bias finish)	½
Optional Folded Border Accent Strip	¼
Border**	2 (seamless) or 1⅛ (pieced)
Backing (pieced crosswise)	3⅛
Binding (cut 2½" strips crosswise)	⅝

*For mirror-image fans as shown, the six-wedge fan is recommended (see page 21).

**For repeats over 18" only, the Main Fabric yardage for the Stack-n-Whack version includes the border. If you would like to use a different fabric, this is the extra yardage you will need, but don't reduce the Main Fabric yardage.

Cutting Stack-n-Whack Wedges

Prepare the main fabric, following the directions on pages 23–29.

Stack-n-Whack Chart for Flip-Flop Fans
Cut layers 21" wide. Cut 5 identical layers for 18° fans, or 6 identical layers for 15° fans.
Use a different set of identical repeats for each additional stack.

If the lengthwise design repeat is:	Use this many design repeats:	Make this many stacks:
6" – 10"	Two repeats per layer	2
11" – 18"	One repeat per layer	2
Over 18"	One repeat per layer	1

Whack...	To make...
(2) 9" strips across width	(15) wedge block kits (8–9 per strip)

Cutting Strip-Cut or Scrap Wedges

Cut 9" wedges, following the instructions starting on page 20. You will need (75) 18° wedges for 5-wedge fans, or (90) 15° wedges for 6-wedge fans.

Cutting Background Fabric	
First Cut	**Second Cut**
(3) 12½" strips across width	(7) 12½" squares (3 per strip)
Remove one selvage	(2) 2½" x 62" and (2) 2½" x 42" lengthwise strips. Set aside for setting strips.
(4) 12½" strips across remaining width	(8) 12½" squares (2 per strip)

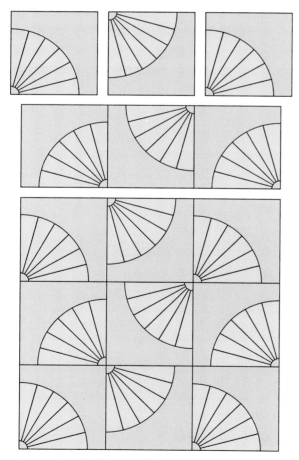

FIGURE 2-2. Quilt assembly.

Making the Blocks

Piece 15 fans, using your choice of techniques. The fan edges in the quilt in the photo are finished with fused bias strips (page 39). Appliqué the fans to the background squares.

Assembling the Quilt Top

Arrange the blocks, following the quilt assembly diagram (Figure 2–2). Sew the vertical seams in each row, then sew the rows together.

Measure the quilt top down the center and trim the two 2½" x 62" strips of background fabric to this length. Sew the strips to the two long sides.

Measure across the width in the center of the quilt. Cut the two 2½" x 42" strips of background fabric to this length. Sew the strips to the top and bottom.

Optional Folded Border Accent Strip

For an inserted accent strip, cut (6) 1¼" strips across the width. Piece the strips together on the diagonal. Press the pieced strip in half lengthwise.

Measure the length of the quilt down the center and cut two insert strips this length. Using a scant ¼" seam, machine baste the strips to the long sides, matching the raw edges.

Measure across the width in the center of the quilt and cut two strips this length. Baste them to the two remaining sides, overlapping the other strips at the corners.

Adding the Borders

The borders have butted corners. Cut (6 or 7) 5" strips across the width and piece to make one long strip, or cut (2) 5" x 67" and (2) 5" x 52" lengthwise strips. Measure the quilt top down the center and cut two borders this length. Sew the borders to the two opposite sides.

Measure across the width in the center of the quilt, including borders, and cut two borders this length. Sew them to the top and bottom.

What if...

I have a lot of blocks?

Add blocks to the width or length of the quilt, rotating the position of the fans in each row in the same alternating pattern (Figure 2–3).

FIGURE 2–3. Flip-Flop variation.

Redwork Ribbons

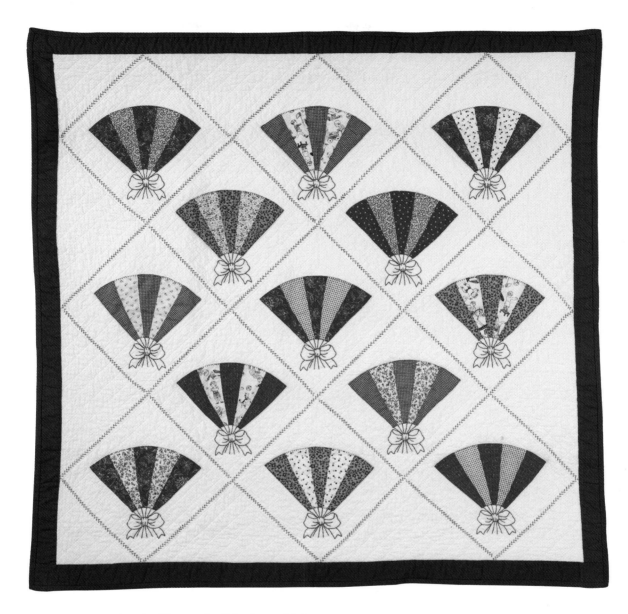

Redwork embroidery by Eleanor Carlisle, Surry, Maine.

Redwork Ribbons

Finished Block Size: 9"
Finished Quilt Top: 41" x 41"
Wedge Length: 5"
Wedge Type: 18° (5 per fan)

R edwork embroidery adds nostalgic charm to these scrap fans. Five-wedge fans work well in the color scheme of two alternating colors, such as the red and white ground prints used in the quilt shown. For a different block size in this setting, use the On-Point Setting reference chart on page 138.

Fabric Requirements
Measurements in yards unless otherwise indicated.

If the design repeat of **Main Fabric** is	6"–10"	11"–14"	15"–17"	18"–26"	over 26"
You will need this many yards for the Stack-n-Whack version: with 18°, 5-wedge fans	1¾	2¼	2⅝	4	5 repeats
with 15°, 6-wedge fans	2	2⅝	3⅛	4⅞	6 repeats
Or, for strip-cut or scrap fan wedges	⅝ yd. or equivalent in scraps				
Additional Fabrics					
Background Fabric	2				
Border	⅜				
Backing (pieced lengthwise)	2⅝				
Binding (cut 2½" strips crosswise)	½				

Cutting Stack-n-Whack Wedges

Prepare the main fabric, following the directions on pages 23–29.

Stack-n-Whack Chart for Redwork Ribbons
Cut layers 21" wide. Cut 5 identical layers for 18° fans, or 6 identical layers for 15° fans. Use a different set of identical repeats for each additional stack.

If the lengthwise design repeat is:	Use this many design repeats:	Make this many stacks:
6" – 11"	One repeat per layer	1*
Over 11"	One repeat per layer	1
Whack…		**To make…**
(1–2) 5" strips across width		(13) wedge block kits
*For 15° wedges, a second stack may be needed. Cut one 5" strip from each stack.		

Strip-Cut or Scrap Version

Cut 5" wedges from assorted fabrics, following the instructions on page 21. For the 13 fans, you will need a total of (65) 15° wedges, or (78) 18° wedges. For alternating colors, as shown in the quilt photo, cut 39 dark and 26 light 15° wedges.

Cutting Background Fabric

For the fan blocks, cut (2) 20" strips across the width of the background fabric. From these strips, cut (3) 20" squares. See Preparing Background Fabric below for additional instructions.

From the remainder of one 20" strip, cut (2) 7¼" squares. Cut each square once on the diagonal to make 8 corner setting triangles. There will be 2 extra triangles.

Cut (1) 14" strip across the fabric width. From this strip, cut (2) 14" squares. Cut each square twice on the diagonal to make 8 side triangles, plus 2 extras. From the remainder of the 14" strip, cut (1) 12" square to make the thirteenth fan block.

Preparing Background Fabric

Before cutting the 20" squares into blocks, you will want to mark and embroider the squares as follows: To create guidelines for placing the embroidery design, fold each 20" square in half vertically and horizontally to divide the squares into quarters, then press the folds. Lightly mark the fold lines with a pencil.

In the full-sized embroidery pattern on page 64, the embroidery lines are shown in red, and the fan placement lines are in black. Lightly trace the embroidery pattern in each quadrant, as shown in Figure 2–4.

To make placement guidelines for the thirteenth square, lightly draw a 9½" square cen-tered on the 12" background piece. Trace the embroidery pattern in one corner. Align the fan seams with the black lines in the pattern.

Making the Blocks

Complete the redwork embroidery by hand or machine. Cut the 20" squares apart on the marked lines and trim all the blocks to 9½" square, measuring from the embroidered corner.

Piece the fans, using your choice of techniques. The quilt in the photo has turned edges that are blanket stitched in place. Using the block placement lines on the embroidery design as a guide, pin the fans to the background fabric, covering the ends of the embroidery design. Appliqué in place.

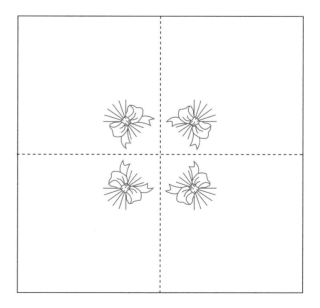

FIGURE 2–4. Trace the embroidery design in each quarter section.

Assembling the Quilt Top

Arrange the fan blocks and setting triangles, following the quilt assembly diagram (Figure 2–5). Sew the seams in each diagonal row, then sew the diagonal rows together.

If desired, add feather stitching or other decorative embroidery to the seam lines by hand or machine.

Adding the Borders

The borders have butted corners. Cut (4) 2" strips across the fabric width. Measure the quilt top down the center and cut two borders this length. Sew the borders to two opposite sides.

Measure across the width in the center of the quilt, including borders, and cut two borders this length. Sew them to the two remaining sides.

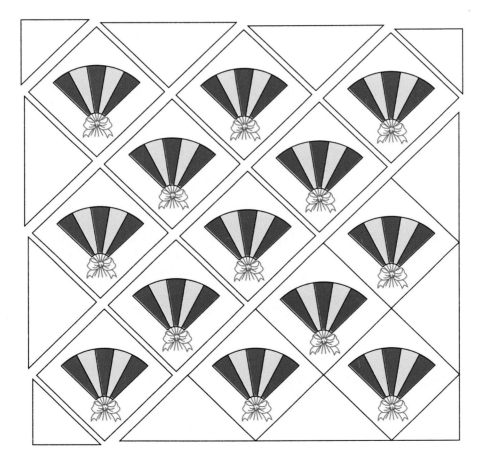

Figure 2-5. Quilt assembly.

What if...

I'd like to use fewer blocks?

For a five-block version, you will need 1 yard of background fabric (Figure 2–6). Use one 20" square plus one 12" square for the blocks. Cut one 14" square twice on the diagonal to make 4 side triangles. Cut (2) 7¼" squares once on the diagonal for the corner setting triangles. Using the same border as the sample, the finished size of this version will be 28½" square.

For a Stack-n-Whack version, a two-color print complements the embroidery (Figure 2–7).

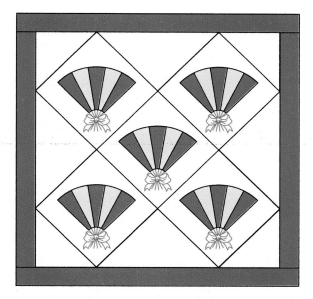

FIGURE 2-6. Redwork Ribbons variation.

FIGURE 2-7. Stack-n-Whack version.

Full-Sized Embroidery Pattern

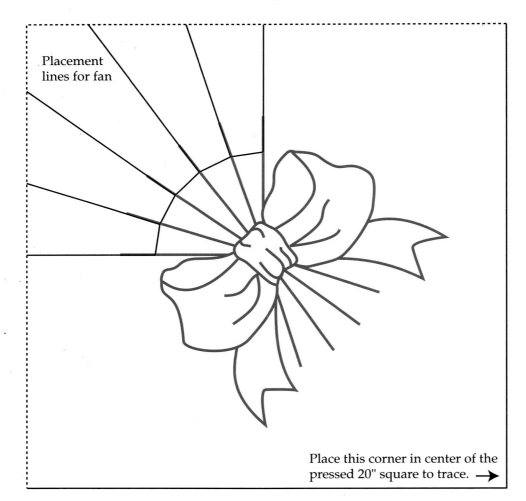

Placement lines for fan

Place this corner in center of the pressed 20" square to trace. →

Rainbows & Rickrack

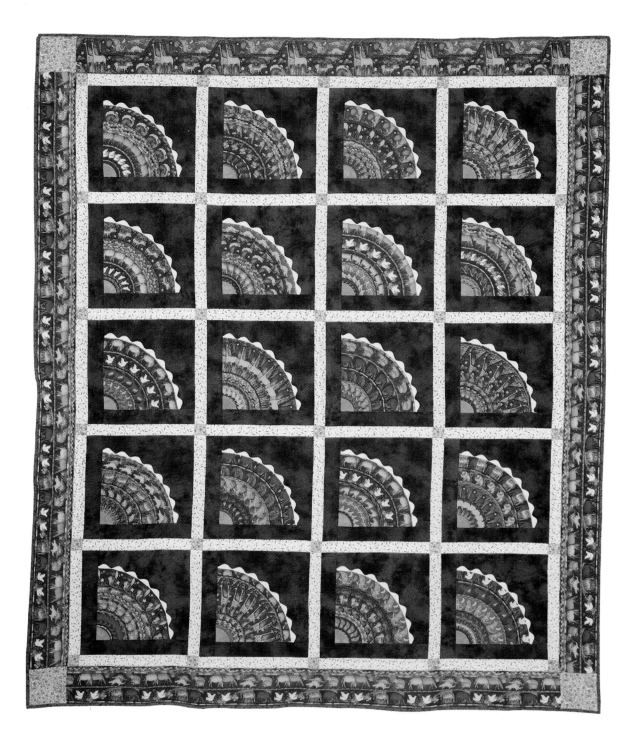

Rainbows & Rickrack

Finished Block Size: 14"
Finished Quilt Top: 72½" x 88"
Wedge Length: 9"
Wedge Type: 15° (6 per fan)

H ere is a quilt as bright and playful as your favorite kid! The striped print creates "rainbows" in each fan, and the optional rickrack trim adds a whimsical note.

Fabric Requirements					
Measurements in yards unless otherwise indicated.					
If the design repeat of **Main Fabric** is	6"–10"	11"–14"	15"–17"	18"–26"	over 26"
You will need this many yards for the Stack-n-Whack version: with 18°, 5-wedge fans	4⅝	4⅜	5¼	4	5 repeats
with 15°, 6-wedge fans (as shown)	5½	5⅛	6¼	4⅞	6 repeats
Or, for strip-cut or scrap fan wedges	2 yds., or equivalent in scraps				
Additional Fabrics					
Background Fabric	3¾				
Fan Bases	¼				
Optional 1" wide Rickrack Trim	10				
Accent Sashing	1⅜				
Cornerstones	¼				
Border*	2½ (seamless) or 1½ (pieced)				
Backing (pieced lengthwise)	5½				
Binding (cut 2½" strips crosswise)	¾				

*For borders as shown, cut seamless strips lengthwise for lengthwise stripes or cut crosswise and piece for crosswise stripes. Allow extra fabric for pattern matching on pieced striped borders.

Cutting the Wedges

Prepare the main fabric, following the directions on pages 23–29. The quilt shown was cut with the Stack-n-Select method.

Stack-n-Select Chart for Rainbows and Rickrack Cut layers 21" wide. Cut 5 identical layers for 18° fans, or 6 identical layers for 15° fans. Use a different set of identical repeats for each additional stack.		
If the lengthwise design repeat is:	**Use this many design repeats:**	**Make this many stacks:**
6" – 10"	Three repeats per layer	2
11" – 18"	Two repeats per layer	2
Over 18"	One repeat per layer	2
Selectively Whack…		
(20) 9" wedge block kits, choosing a different part of the fabric design for each kit.		

Stack-n-Whack Chart for Rainbows and Rickrack Cut layers 21" wide. Cut 5 identical layers for 18° fans, or 6 identical layers for 15° fans. Use a different set of identical repeats for each additional stack.		
If the lengthwise design repeat is:	**Use this many design repeats:**	**Make this many stacks:**
6" – 10"	Three repeats for first stack, and two repeats for second stack	2
11" – 18"	Two repeats for first stack, and one repeat for second stack	2
Over 18"	One repeat for each stack	2
Whack…		**To make…**
(3) 9" strips across width		(20) wedge block kits (8–9 per strip)

Cutting Strip-Cut or Scrap Wedges

Cut 9" wedges, following the instructions starting on page 20. You will need (100) 18° wedges for 5-wedge fans, or (120) 15° wedges for 6-wedge fans.

Cutting Background Fabric	
First Cut	**Second Cut**
(7) 12½" strips across width	(20) 12½" squares
(10) 2½" strips across width	(20) 2½" x 14½" rectangles (2 per strip) and (10) 2½" x 12½" rectangles (1 from the remainder of each strip)
(4) 2½" strips across width	(10) 2½" x 12½" rectangles (3 per strip)

Making the Blocks

Piece 20 fans, using your choice of techniques. The quilt in the photo has rickrack trim finish (page 40) and fused machine appliquéd quarter-circle bases (page 44). Appliqué the fans to the background squares.

For the fused fan bases, prepare (5) 3½" circles (page 133), and cut to make 20 quarter-circles. Appliqué the bases to the fan blocks.

Add a 2½" x 12½" background fabric strip to the left of each fan, as shown in Figure 2–8. Add a 2½" x 14½" strip to the bottom of each fan to complete the block.

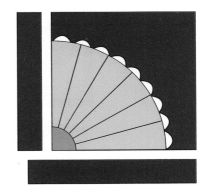

FIGURE 2-8. Add background strips to the block.

Cutting Accent Sashing and Cornerstones		
Fabric	**First Cut**	**Second Cut**
Accent Sashing	(3) 14½" strips across width	(49) 2" x 14½" rectangles
Sashing Cornerstones	(2) 2" strips across width	(30) 2" squares
Border Cornerstones	(1) 5" strips across width	(4) 5" squares

Assembling the Quilt Top

Arrange the sashed fan blocks, accent sashing, and cornerstones, following the quilt assembly diagram (Figure 2–9). Sew the vertical seams in each row, then sew the rows together.

Adding the Borders

Note that these measurements are for borders cut 5" wide, but if you are using a striped border, you may want to adjust this width to suit your fabric.

For stripes printed lengthwise, measure the quilt top down the center and cut two 5"-wide strips this length, parallel to the selvages. Sew the borders to the two long sides. Measure across the width in the center of the quilt, including the borders. Cut two 5"-wide strips this length, also parallel to the selvages. Sew a cornerstone to each end of both strips. Sew the border-cornerstone strips to the top and bottom.

For stripes printed crosswise or other directional fabrics, cut (8) 5" strips across the width. (For striped fabrics, if you allow extra length for matching the print, you can trim between cuts so that the stripes will match when the border strips are joined end to end.) Piece strips together in pairs. Measure the quilt top down the center and cut two of the strips this length. Sew them to the two long sides. Measure across the width in the center of the quilt, including the borders. Cut two strips this length. Sew a cornerstone to each end of both strips. Sew the border-cornerstone strips to the top and bottom.

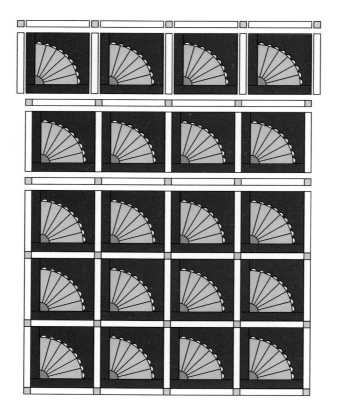

Figure 2-9. Quilt assembly.

What if...

I have a directional print, and I don't want any of the motifs to be upside down?

You may be able to selectively cut enough block kits to keep the designs running consistently in one direction. Or, consider using a different layout. By rotating some of the blocks, you can get upside-down animals back on their feet (Figure 2–10)!

FIGURE 2-10. Blocks with directional patterns can be rotated to keep the patterns running the same direction.

Framed Fans

Framed Fans

Finished Block Size: 8" (including frame)

Finished Quilt Top: 38" x 38"

Wedge Length: 6"

Wedge Type Shown: 15° (6 per fan)

A narrow frame around the fan block separates the fan from the print used in the alternate blocks and gives each block more definition. The fans shown here were selectively cut from a symmetrical print. Directions for this cutting technique are on page 29.

To use this setting with a different block size, use the On-Point Setting reference chart on page 138. Include the frame in the finished block measurement when determining the sizes for the setting pieces.

Fabric Requirements Measurements in yards unless otherwise indicated.					
If the design repeat of **Main Fabric** is	7"–10"	11"–14"	15"–17"	18"–26"	over 26"
You will need this many yards for the Stack-n-Whack version: with 18°, 5-wedge fans (as shown)	1¾ or 3⅛*	2¼	2⅝	4	5 repeats
with 15°, 6-wedge fans	2 or 3¾*	2⅝	3⅛	4⅞	6 repeats
Or, for strip-cut or scrap fan wedges	⅝ yd. or equivalent in scraps				
Additional Fabrics					
Background Fabric	⅝				
Fan Accent Fabric (fan bases optional)	¼				
Narrow Sashing	⅜				
Setting Fabric (alternate blocks)	¾				
Backing	1¼				
Binding (cut 2½" strips crosswise)	⅜				
*For symmetrical prints, use the higher yardage figure to allow for selective cutting.					

Cutting the Wedges

Prepare the main fabric, following the directions on pages 23–29. The quilt shown was cut with the Stack-n-Select method.

Stack-n-Select Chart for Framed Fans
Cut layers 21" wide. Cut 5 identical layers for 18° fans, or 6 identical layers for 15° fans.
Use a different set of identical repeats for each additional stack.

If the lengthwise design repeat is:	Use this many design repeats:	Make this many stacks:
6"–11"	Two repeats per layer	2
Over 11"	One repeat per layer	2

Selectively Whack...

(9) 6" wedge block kits, choosing a different part of the fabric design for each kit.

Stack-n-Whack Chart for Framed Fans
Cut layers 21" wide. Cut 5 identical layers for 18° fans, or 6 identical layers for 15° fans.
Use a different set of identical repeats for each additional stack.

If the lengthwise design repeat is:	Use this many design repeats:	Make this many stacks:
Over 6"	One repeat per layer	1

Whack...	To make...
(1) 6" strip across the width	(9) wedge block kits

Cutting Strip-Cut or Scrap Wedges

Cut 6" wedges, following the instructions starting on page 20. You will need (45) 18° wedges for 5-wedge fans, or (54) 15° wedges for 6-wedge fans.

Cutting Background, Frame, and Setting Fabrics		
Fabric	**First Cut**	**Second Cut**
Background	(2) 7½" strips across width	(9) 7½" squares (5 per strip)
Frames	(9) 1" strips across width	(18) 1" x 7½" strips and (18) 1" x 8½" strips
Setting (alternate blocks)	(1) 8½" strips across width	(4) 8½" squares for alternate blocks
Setting (side triangles)	(2) 12⅝" squares	Cut each square twice on the diagonal to make (8) side triangles
Setting (corner triangles)	(2) 6⅝" squares	Cut each square once on the diagonal to make (4) corner triangles

Making the Blocks and Adding Frames

Piece 9 fans, using your choice of techniques. The sample quilt has pointed wedges (page 31) and cording (page 40).

Appliqué fans to the 7½" background fabric squares. The sample quilt has a pressed-under edge at the inner curve (page 36). If you prefer to add fan bases, prepare (3) 3" circles (page 133) and cut them into 4 quarter-circles. Appliqué the quarter-circle fan bases in place.

Sew a 1" x 7½" strip to two opposite sides of each fan block. Press the seam allowances away from the block and sew a 1" x 8½" strip to the other two sides of each block.

Assembling the Quilt Top

Arrange the fan blocks, setting squares, and setting triangles, following the quilt assembly diagram. Sew the seams in each diagonal row, then sew the diagonal rows together (Figure 2–11).

What if...

I use scrap fabrics for the wedges?

Scrap fans are quite attractive in this setting, as you can see in Figure 2–12.

FIGURE 2-12. Reproduction prints complement the vintage 1860s floral used in the alternate blocks.

FIGURE 2-11. Quilt assembly.

Very Victorian

Very Victorian

    Finished Block Size: 10"; 12½" with sashing and cornerstones

    Finished Quilt Top: 62" x 62"

    Wedge Length: 8"

    Wedge Type Shown: 18° (5 per fan)

The Stack-n-Whack fan wedges get their symmetry from the mirror-image trick. See page 30 for information on this optional technique. Scalloped edges and appliquéd corner-stones add interest to this classic medallion setting.

Fabric Requirements
Measurements in yards unless otherwise indicated.

If the design repeat of **Main Fabric** is	6"–10"	11"–14"	15"–17"	18"–26"	over 26"
You will need this many yards for the Stack-n-Whack version*: with 18°, 5-wedge fans	3⅛	2¼	2⅝	4	5 repeats
with 15°, 6-wedge fans (as shown)	3¾	2⅝	3⅛	4⅞	6 repeats
Or, for strip-cut or scrap fan wedges	1⅜ yds. or equivalent in scraps				

Additional Fabrics	
Background	2⅜
Fan Bases and Cornerstone Appliqué	⅜
Inner Border – pieced	½
Outer Border**	2 (seamless) or 1 (pieced)
Backing (pieced crosswise)	4
Binding (cut 2½" strips crosswise)	⅝

* For mirror-image fans as shown, the six-wedge fan is recommended (see page 21).

**For repeats over 18", the Main Fabric yardage for the Stack-n-Whack version includes the border. If you would like to use a different fabric, this is the extra yardage you will need, but don't reduce the Main Fabric yardage.

Cutting Stack-n-Whack Wedges

Prepare the main fabric, following the directions on pages 23–29.

Stack-n-Whack Chart for Very Victorian		
Cut layers 21" wide. Cut 5 identical layers for 18° fans, or 6 identical layers for 15° fans. Use a different set of identical repeats for each additional stack.		
If the lengthwise design repeat is:	Use this many design repeats:	Make this many stacks:
6" – 10"	Two repeats per layer	2
11" – 18"	One repeat per layer	2
Over 18"	One repeat per layer	1
Whack...		To make...
(2) 8" strips across the width		(16) wedge block kits (8–9 per strip)

Cutting Strip-Cut or Scrap Wedges

Cut 8" wedges, following the instructions starting on page 20. You will need (80) 18° wedges for 5-wedge fans, or (96) 15° wedges for 6-wedge fans.

Cutting Background Fabric	
First Cut	Second Cut
(4) 10½" strips across width	(16) 10½" squares
(3) 10½" strips across width	(32) 3 x 10½" strips and (16) 3" squares

Making the Blocks

Piece 16 fans, using your choice of techniques. The quilt in the photo has scalloped wedges (page 33) and appliquéd quarter-circle bases (page 41). Appliqué the fans to the background squares.

For the fan bases and cornerstone appliqués, prepare (8) 5" circles (pattern on page 133) and cut to make 32 quarter-circles (circle patterns on page 133).

Figure 2-13. Add sashing strips and a cornerstone to each fan block.

Appliqué the bases to the fan blocks. Appliqué the remaining quarter-circles to the 3" squares to make the 16 cornerstones.

Lay out each block with two sashing strips and a cornerstone, as shown in Figure 2–13. Piece together to complete the sashed block unit.

Assembling the Quilt Top

Arrange the sashed fan blocks, following the quilt assembly diagram (Figure 2–14). Sew the vertical seams in each row, then sew the rows together.

Adding the Borders

The borders have butted corners. For the inner border, cut (5) 2" strips across the width of the fabric. Piece the strips together to make one long strip. For the outer border, cut (7) 5" strips across the width. Piece the strips together to make one long strip, or cut (4) 5" x 64" lengthwise strips.

Measure the quilt top down the center and cut two inner borders this length. Sew the borders to two opposite sides.

Measure across the width in the center of the quilt, including borders, and cut two inner borders this length. Sew them to the two remaining sides. Repeat these steps for the outer border.

What if...

I rotate some of the blocks?

Rotating several of the blocks can produce various designs (Figure 2–15).

Figure 2-14. Quilt assembly.

Figure 2-15. Very Victorian variation.

Friendship Fans

Friendship Fans

Finished Block Size: 8"
Finished Quilt Top: 35" x 48"
Wedge Length: 7"
Wedge Type Shown: 18° (5 per fan)

Australian wildflower fabrics, given to me from friends "down under," inspired this design. Two colorways of the same print alternate in the fans. Whenever you use fabrics from two different bolts in the same stack, check before cutting to be sure the repeats match in both length and width. Lay a corner of one fabric on top of the other to check the design alignment.

Fabric Requirements
Measurements in yards unless otherwise indicated.

If the design repeat of **Main Fabric** is	6"–10"	11"–14"	15"–17"	18"–26"	over 26"
You will need this many yards for the Stack-n-Whack version with 2 colors: 18°, 5-wedge fans (as shown)	2 (A) and 1⅜ (B)	1½ (A) and 1⅛ (B)	1¾ (A) and 1¼ (B)	2½ (A) and 1⅞ (B)	3 repeats (A) and 2 repeats (B)
with one-color, 15°, 6-wedge fans	3	2⅝	3⅛	4⅞	6 repeats
Or, for strip-cut or scrap fan wedges	¾ yd. or equivalent in scraps				
Additional Fabrics					
Background	⅞				
Accent (fan bases, cornerstones)	¼				
Setting (side and corner triangles)	¾				
Inner Border	¼				
Outer Border*	1⅜ (seamless) or ½ (pieced)				
Backing	1½				
Binding (cut 2½" strips crosswise)	½				

*The Main Fabric A yardage for the Stack-n-Whack version includes the border. If you would like to use a different fabric, this is the extra yardage you will need, but don't reduce the Main Fabric yardage.

Cutting Stack-n-Whack Wedges

Prepare the main fabric, following the directions on pages 23–29.

Stack-n-Whack Chart for Friendship Fans		
Cut layers 21" wide. Cut 5 identical layers for 18° fans, or 6 identical layers for 15° fans. Use a different set of identical repeats for each additional stack.		
If the lengthwise design repeat is:	**Use this many design repeats:**	**Make this many stacks:**
6" – 8"	Two repeats per layer	1
Over 8"	One repeat per layer	1
*For the two-color version shown, cut 3 layers from Fabric A and 2 layers from Fabric B for 18° fans, or 3 layers from each fabric for 15° fans.		
Whack...		**To make...**
(1) 7" strip across the width		(8) wedge block kits

Cutting Strip-Cut or Scrap Wedges

Cut 7" wedges, following the instructions starting on page 20. You will need (40) 18° wedges for 5-wedge fans, or (48) 15° wedges for 6-wedge fans.

Cutting Background, Cornerstone, and Setting Fabrics		
Fabric	**First Cut**	**Second Cut**
Background	(2) 8½" strips across width	(8) 8½" squares (4 per strip)
Background	(6) 1½" strips across width	(24) 1½" x 8½" sashing strips
Accent	(1) 1½" strips across width	(17) 1½" squares
Setting (side triangles)	(2) 14" squares	Cut each square twice on the diagonal to make (6) side triangles, plus 2 extras
Setting (corner triangles)	(2) 8" squares	Cut each square once on the diagonal to make (4) corner triangles

Making the Blocks

Piece 8 fans, using your choice of techniques. The quilt in the photo has pointed wedges (page 31) and appliquéd quarter-circle bases (page 41).

Appliqué the fans to the background squares. Prepare (2) 3" circles (page 133) and cut to make 8 quarter-circles. Appliqué the bases to the fan blocks.

Assembling the Quilt Top

Lay out the blocks, sashing strips, cornerstones, and setting triangles as shown in the quilt assembly diagram (Figure 2–16). Note that the sections must be assembled in the order shown for the setting triangles to fit correctly.

Figure 2-16. Quilt assembly.

Adding the Borders

If you are using a directional fabric, such as the print in the quilt in the photo, you may want to cut two borders lengthwise and two crosswise to keep the design running one way. Piece as needed.

The borders have butted corners. For the inner border, cut (4) 1½" strips across the width. For the outer border, cut (2) 3½" x 37" and (2) 3½" x 44" lengthwise strips, or cut (4) 3½" strips across the width. For strips cut across the width of the fabric, sew them together end to end.

Measure the quilt top down the center and cut two inner borders this length. Sew the borders to two opposite sides.

Measure across the width in the center of the quilt, including borders, and cut two borders this length. Sew them to the top and bottom. Repeat for the outer border.

What if...

I use the bias-edge finish instead of the pointed wedges?

Wedges finished with the bias-edge technique will be slightly larger than the same-sized wedges finished with a pointed or scalloped edge. In this design, 7" wedges would be too crowded on 8" background squares. For more attractive proportions, use 6" wedges for the bias-edge finish and keep the other measurements the same (Figure 2–17, page 87).

FIGURE 2-17a AND b. Bias-edged fans with 7" wedges are too big for an 8" block. Reducing the fan wedges to 6" is the answer.

Sugar & Spice

Sugar & Spice

Finished Block Size: 6"
Finished Quilt Top: 42" x 42"
Wedge Length: 5"
Wedge Type: 15° (6 per fan)

few strategically placed reds add the spice to this sweet collection of reproduction 30s prints. This project would be perfect for a wall quilt or baby bunting.

Fabric Requirements
Measurements in yards unless otherwise indicated.

If the design repeat of **Main Fabric** is	6"–10"	11"–14"	15"–17"	18"–26"	over 26"
You will need this many yards for the Stack-n-Whack version: with 18°, 5-wedge fans	3⅛	2¼	2⅝	4	5 repeats
with 15°, 6-wedge fans	3¾	2⅝	3⅛	4⅞	6 repeats
Or, for strip-cut or scrap fan wedges	1⅜ yds. or equivalent in scraps				
Additional Fabrics					
Background Fabric and Second Border	1⅜				
Fan Bases	¼				
First and Third Borders	½				
Backing (pieced lengthwise)	2⅝				
Binding (cut 2½" strip crosswise)	½				

Cutting Stack-n-Whack Wedges

Prepare the main fabric, following the directions on pages 23–29.

Stack-n-Whack Chart for Sugar and Spice
Cut layers 21" wide. Cut 5 identical layers for 18° fans, or 6 identical layers for 15° fans.
Use a different set of identical repeats for each additional stack.

If the lengthwise design repeat is:	Use this many design repeats:	Make this many stacks:
6" – 10"	Two repeats per layer	2
11" – 21"	One repeat per layer	2
Over 21"	One repeat per layer	1
Whack...		**To make...**
(4) 5" strips across width		(36) wedge block kits (11–13 per strip)

Cutting Strip-Cut or Scrap Wedges

Cut 5" wedges, following the instructions starting on page 20. You will need (180) 18° wedges for 5-wedge fans, or (216) 15° wedges for 6-wedge fans.

Cutting Background Fabric	
First Cut	**Second Cut**
(1) 12½" strip across width	(1) 12½" square and (4) 6½" x 12½" rectangles
(4) 6½" strips across width	(24) 6½" squares
(4) 1½" strips across width	Set aside for borders

Making the Blocks

Piece the fans, using your choice of techniques. The quilt in the photo has folded points (page 31) and appliquéd bases.

Piece (24) 15° wedges or (20) 18° wedges for the center block. Appliqué the pieced wedges to the 12½" background square.

Piece 4 half-circle fans, using (12) 15° wedges or (10) 18° wedges for each. Appliqué the pieced wedges to the 6½" x 12½" background rectangles.

Piece 24 fans and appliqué them to the 6½" background squares.

For fan bases, prepare (6) 3½" circles (pattern on page 133) and cut to make 24 quarter-circles. Appliqué the bases to the 6" fan blocks.

Prepare one 3" circle. Appliqué it in place on the center square. Prepare (4) 3½" half-circles. Appliqué them in place on the half-circle blocks.

Assembling the Quilt Top

Arrange the fan blocks, following the quilt assembly diagram (Figure 2–18). Sew the vertical seams in each row, then sew the rows together.

FIGURE 2-18. Quilt assembly.

FIGURE 2-19. SUGAR & SPICE variation.

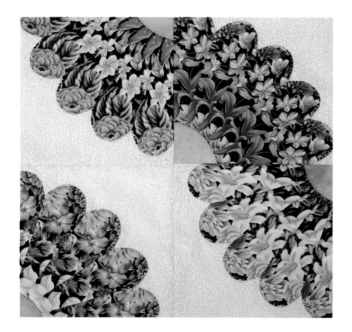

FIGURE 2-20. Stack-n-Whack version.

Adding the Borders

The borders have butted corners. Cut (9) 1½" strips across the width for the first and third border. Measure the quilt top down the center and cut two borders this length. Sew the borders to two opposite sides.

Measure across the width in the center of the quilt, including borders, and cut two borders this length. Sew them to the two remaining sides.

Repeat for the second border, using the 1½" background fabric strips. Repeat for the third border, using the four remaining strips of border fabric.

The pattern for the heart quilting motif shown in the sample is given below.

What if...

I rotate the fan blocks?

Rotating the fan blocks can create various quilt designs (Figure 2–19).

The Stack-n-whack version shown in Figure 2–20 has a scalloped edge finish.

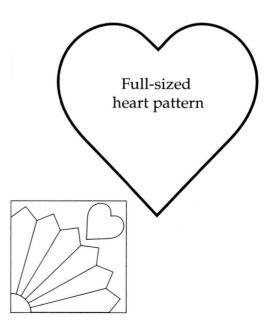

Full-sized
heart pattern

Fan Sampler

Fan Sampler

Finished Block Size: 10"
Finished Quilt Top: 53" x 53"
Wedge Length: 8"
Wedge Types Shown: 18° (5 per fan), 15° (6 per fan)

S ashing helps to unify the diverse blocks in this teaching sampler. You can use any combination of techniques and wedge types, or use this setting to feature just one style of block.

Fabric Requirements					
Measurements in yards unless otherwise indicated.					
If the design repeat of **Main Fabric** is	6"–10"	11"–14"	15"–17"	18"–26"	over 26"
You will need this many yards for the Stack-n-Whack version: with 18°, 5-wedge fans only	3⅛	2¼	2⅝	4	5 repeats
with 15°, 6-wedge fans, or both types	3¾	2⅝	3⅛	4⅞	6 repeats
Or, for strip-cut or scrap fan wedges	1⅛ yd. or equivalent in scraps				
Additional Fabrics					
Background Fabric	1¾				
Fan Accent Fabric (single bias finish, bases)	⅜				
Sashing	⅝				
Border*	1¾ (seamless) or 1 (pieced)				
Backing (pieced lengthwise)	3½				
Binding (cut 2½" strips crosswise)	⅝				
*For repeats over 18" only, the Main Fabric yardage for the Stack-n-Whack version includes the border. If you would like to use a different fabric, this is the extra yardage you will need, but don't reduce the Main Fabric yardage.					

Cutting Stack-n-Whack Wedges

Prepare the main fabric, following the directions on pages 23–29.

Stack-n-Whack Chart for Fan Sampler		
Cut layers 21" wide. Cut 5 identical layers for 18° fans, or 6 identical layers for 15° fans. Use a different set of identical repeats for each additional stack.		
If the lengthwise design repeat is:	**Use this many design repeats:**	**Make this many stacks:**
6" – 10"	Two repeats per layer	2
11" – 18"	One repeat per layer	2
Over 18"	One repeat per layer	1
Whack…		**To make…**
(2) 8" strips across width		(14) wedge block kits (8–9 per strip)

Cutting Strip-Cut or Scrap Wedges

Cut 8" wedges, following the instructions starting on page 20. You will need (80) 18° wedges for 5-wedge fans, or (96) 15° wedges for 6-wedge fans.

Cutting Background and Sashing Fabrics		
Fabric	**First Cut**	**Second Cut**
Background	(3) 10½" strips across width	(12) 10½" squares (4 per strip)
Background	(1) 21½" strips across width	(1) 21½" square
Background	(2) 8" squares from the remainder of the 21½" strip	(10) 18° or (12) 15° wedges for center circle
*Sashing	(10) 1½" strips across width	(8) 1½" x 10½" strips
*Piece the 7 remaining strips to make one long strip. From that strip, cut (4) 1½" x 43½" and (2) 1½" x 45½" sashing strips.		

Making the Blocks

Piece 12 fans and one full circle fan, using your choice of techniques. For the bias-edge finish shown on some blocks in the photo, cut an 11" strip across the width of the fan accent fabric, and cut into 1¼" bias strips.

The center block in the sample is made from two alternating block kits, with wedges of background fabric between the main fabric wedges. Appliqué the fans and circle to the background squares.

Add a 3" circle center and 3" quarter-circle fan bases, following the instructions on page 41 (circle patterns on page 133).

Assembling the Quilt Top

Arrange the blocks and sashing strips, following the quilt assembly diagram (Figure 2–21). Attach the sashing strips in the order shown. Sew the vertical seams in each row, then sew the rows together.

Adding the Borders

If you are using a directional fabric, such as the print in the sample quilt, you may want to cut two borders lengthwise and two crosswise to keep the design running one way. Piece the border strips as needed to obtain the required length.

The borders have butted corners. Cut (2) 4½" x 46" and (2) 4½" x 54" lengthwise strips, or cut (6) 4½" strips across the width and piece to make one long strip.

Measure the quilt top down the center and cut two borders this length. Sew the borders to two opposite sides.

Measure across the width in the center of the quilt, including borders, and cut two borders this length. Sew them to the top and bottom.

What if...

I use four fan blocks in the center, instead of a circle?

Cut two more 1½" x 10½" strips and one more 1½" x 21½" strip from the sashing fabric. Try rotating the fans for different effects (Figure 2–22).

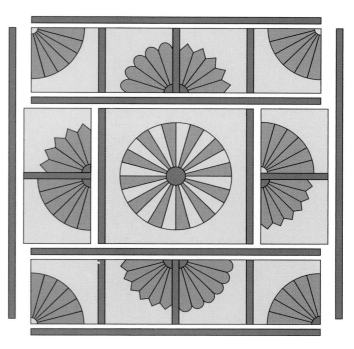

FIGURE 2-21. Quilt assembly.

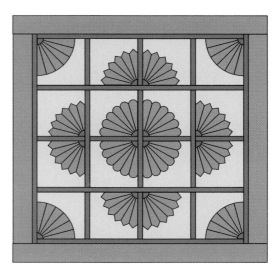

FIGURE 2-22. FAN SAMPLER variation.

Lazy Daisies

Lazy Daisies

Finished Block Size: 14"

Finished Quilt Top: 56" x 70"

Wedge Length: 5"

Wedge Type Shown: 18° (20 per fan)

lternating wedges cut from the background and border fabrics make these sprightly blooms seem to float over the surface of the quilt.

Fabric Requirements Measurements in yards unless otherwise indicated.					
If the design repeat of **Main Fabric** is	6"–10"	11"–14"	15"–17"	18"–26"	over 26"
You will need this many yards for the Stack-n-Whack version: with 18°, 20-wedge circles (as shown)	3⅛	4⅜	5¼	8	10 repeats
with 15°, 24-wedge circles	3¾	5⅛	6¼	9⅝	12 repeats
Or, for strip-cut or scrap fan wedges	1½ yds. or equivalent in scraps				
Additional Fabrics					
Background Fabric	3⅝				
Accent Fabric (block centers)	¼				
Border	2¼				
Backing (pieced crosswise)	3½				
Binding (cut 2½" strips crosswise)	⅝				

Cutting Stack-n-Whack Wedges

Prepare the main fabric, following the directions on pages 23–29.

Stack-n-Whack Chart for Lazy Daisies Cut layers 21" wide. Cut 10 identical layers for 18° fans, or 12 identical layers for 15° fans. Use a different set of identical repeats for each additional stack.		
If the lengthwise design repeat is:	Use this many design repeats:	Make this many stacks:
Under 10"	One repeat per layer	2
Over 11"	One repeat per layer	1
Whack…		**To make…**
(2) 5" strips across width		(20) wedge block kits (10–13 per strip)

Cutting Strip-Cut or Scrap Wedges

Cut 5" wedges, following the instructions starting on page 21. You will need (200) 18° wedges for 20-wedge circles, or (240) 15° wedges for 24-wedge circles.

Cutting Background and Border Fabrics		
Fabric	**First Cut**	**Second Cut**
Background	(3) 14½" strips across width	(6) 14½" squares and (3) 7½" x 14½" rectangles (2 squares and 1 rectangle per strip)
Background	(3) 14½" strips across width	(7) 7½" x 14½" rectangles and (4) 7½" squares
Background	(6) 5" strips across width	(120) 18° wedges, or (144) 15° wedges
Border	(3) 14½" strips across width	(14) 7½" x 14½" rectangles
Border	(1) 7½" strip across width	(4) 7½" squares
Border	(4) 5" strips across width	(80) 18° wedges, or (96) 15° wedges

Preparing the Border Blocks

Piece together pairs of 7½" x 14½" background and border rectangles to make (10) 14½" square side border blocks.

For the corner blocks, piece 4 pairs of 7½" background and border squares, then sew these to the remaining rectangles of border fabric to make 14½" corner blocks.

Making the Circle Blocks

Piece 20 circles. For the 6 center circles, alternate main fabric and background fabric wedges. For the border blocks, alternate main background and border fabric wedges. Refer to Figure 2–23 for fabric placement.

Press under ¼" of the outer raw edge of the circles. Appliqué the center circles to the (6) 14½" background squares. Appliqué the border circles to the pieced border blocks, aligning the seam lines between the wedges with the seam lines of the pieced blocks (Figure 2–23). Change thread colors as necessary to blend with the background and border fabrics.

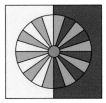

Side borders
Make 6

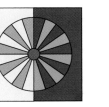

Top and bottom borders
Make 4

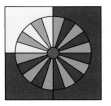

Upper left and lower right corners
Make 2

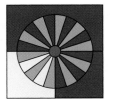

Upper right and lower left corners
Make 2

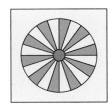

Center blocks
Make 6

FIGURE 2-23. Lazy Daisy blocks.

FIGURE 2–24. Quilt assembly.

Prepare (20) 2" circles for block bases, and appliqué the bases in place (circle patterns on page 133).

Assembling the Quilt Top

Arrange the blocks, following the quilt assembly diagram (Figure 2–24). Sew the vertical seams in each row, then sew the rows together.

What if...

I want to use less than 10 or 12 repeats?

This block is also interesting when made with two alternating 5-layer or 6-layer Stack-n-Whack block kits. If the two kits paired in the block are clearly different, the effect can be striking (Figure 2–25).

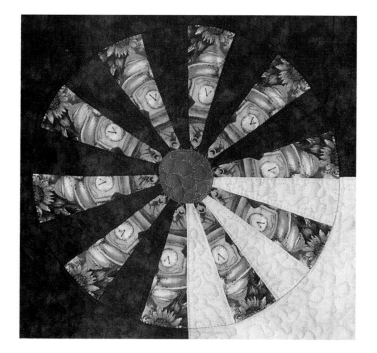

LAZY DAISIES corner detail.

FIGURE 2–25. LAZY DAISIES variation.

F or the LAZY DAISIES variation, use the following main fabric yardages and cutting instructions:

Fabric Requirements
Measurements in yards unless otherwise indicated.

If the design repeat of **Main Fabric** is	6"–10"	11"–14"	15"–17"	18"–26"	over 26"
You will need this many yards for the Stack-n-Whack version: with 18°, 20-wedge circles (5 layers)	3⅛	2¼	2⅝	4	5 repeats
with 15°, 24-wedge circles (6 layers)	3¾	2⅝	3⅛	4⅞	6 repeats

Cutting Stack-n-Whack Wedges

Prepare the main fabric, following the directions on pages 23–29.

Stack-n-Whack Chart for Lazy Daisies Variation
Cut layers 21" wide. Cut 5 identical layers for 18° fans, or 6 identical layers for 15° fans. Use a different set of identical repeats for each additional stack.

If the lengthwise design repeat is:	Use this many design repeats:	Make this many stacks:
Under 11"	Two repeats per layer	2
11" – 21"	One repeat per layer	2
Over 21"	One repeat per layer	1
Whack...		**To make...**
(4) 5" strips across width		(40) wedge block kits (10–13 per strip). You will use two block kits for each circle.

Lay out each block before piecing it, alternating two block kits and filling in between the block kit wedges with the background and/or border fabric wedges.

Full Plates

Full Plates

Finished Block Size: 15"
Finished Quilt Top: 61" x 61"
Wedge Length: 6"
Wedge Type Shown: 18° (20 per fan)

Two block kits alternate in each block to create intricate new patterns.

Fabric Requirements
Measurements in yards unless otherwise indicated.

If the design repeat of **Main Fabric** is	7"–10"	11"–14"	15"–17"	18"–26"	over 26"
You will need this many yards for the Stack-n-Whack version: with 18°, 20-wedge circles (as shown)	3⅛	4⅜	5¼*	8*	10 repeats*
with 15°, 24-wedge circles	3¾	5⅛	6¼*	9⅝*	12 repeats*
Or, for strip-cut or scrap fan wedges	1⅞ yds. or equivalent in scraps				

Additional Fabrics	
Background Fabric	3⅞
Accent Fabric (block centers)	¼
Inner Border	⅜
Backing (pieced crosswise)	4
Binding (cut 2½" strips crosswise)	⅝

*See What If? (page 108) regarding these yardages.

Cutting Stack-n-Whack Wedges

Prepare the main fabric, following the directions on pages 23–29.

Stack-n-Whack Chart for Full Plates
Cut layers 21" wide. Cut 10 identical layers for 18° fans, or 12 identical layers for 15° fans.
Use a different set of identical repeats for each additional stack.

If the lengthwise design repeat is:	Use this many design repeats:	Make this many stacks:
Under 14"	One repeat per layer	2
Over 14"	One repeat per layer	1

Whack...	To make...
(2) 6" strips across width	(20) wedge block kits (10–11 per strip) You will use two block kits for each circle.

Cutting Strip-Cut or Scrap Wedges

Cut 6" wedges, following the instructions starting on page 20. You will need (200) 18° wedges for 20-wedge circles, or (240) 15° wedges for 24-wedge circles.

Cutting Background Fabric	
First Cut	**Second Cut**
(5) 15½" strips across width	(9) 15½" squares (2 per strip)
Remove one selvage	(7) 7¼" x 47" lengthwise strips. Set aside for outer border
From the remaining fabric, cut (4) 8½" squares for the corner blocks.	

Making the Blocks

For the Stack-n-Whack version shown, use 2 sets of 10 or 12 wedges for each circle. Use 2 sets to make the corner fan blocks, alternating 3 from one set and 2 from the second set in each fan for the 18° version, or 3 from each set for the 15° version.

Piece 9 circles and 4 fans, using your choice of techniques. The sample quilt has pointed wedges (page 31) and appliquéd centers and quarter-circle bases (page 41). Appliqué the circles to the 15½" background fabric squares. Prepare (9) 2½"circles (pattern on page 133) for the block centers, and appliqué the center circles in place. Appliqué the fans to the 8½" background squares.

Prepare one 3" circle and cut into 4 quarter-circles. Appliqué the quarter-circle fan bases in place.

Assembling the Quilt Top

Arrange the center blocks, following the quilt assembly diagram (Figure 2–26, page 108). Sew the vertical seams in each row, then sew the rows together.

From the inner border fabric, cut (5) 1¾" strips across the width from the narrow border fabric. Piece the strips together to make one long strip. Cut (4) 47" strips from the long strip. Piece one strip to each of the 7¼" x 47" background fabric strips.

Measure the quilt top down the center and trim the pieced borders to this length. Piece two borders to the sides of the quilt.

Following the quilt assembly diagram, piece a fan block to each end of the two remaining borders. Piece the fan block-border units to the top and bottom of the quilt.

Figure 2-26. Quilt assembly

Full Plates corner detail.

What if...

I have a print with a large repeat, and I want to use less yardage?

For repeats over 14", you can reduce the main fabric yardage substantially by using repeats from both sides of the fabric in the 10 or 12 layer stack. For this variation, use the following main fabric yardages and cutting instructions.

F or the FULL PLATES variation, use the following main fabric yardages and cutting instructions:

Fabric Requirements
Measurements in yards unless otherwise indicated.

If the design repeat of **Main Fabric** is	15"–17"	18"–26"	over 26"
You will need this many yards for the Stack-n-Whack version: with 18°, 20-wedge circles (as shown)	2⅝	4	5 repeats
with 15°, 24-wedge circles	3⅛	4⅞	6 repeats

Cutting Stack-n-Whack Wedges

Prepare the main fabric, following the directions on pages 23–29.

Stack-n-Whack Chart for Full Plates Variation
From one half-width of fabric (approx. 21" wide), cut 5 identical layers for 18° fans, or 6 identical layers for 15° fans. Using one of these layers, find and cut the matching portion of the print on the other half-width. This new piece may only match on part of the 21" width. Use this new piece to cut the remaining layers. You will need a total of 10 layers for 18° fans, or 12 layers for 15° fans.

If the lengthwise design repeat is:	Use this many design repeats:	Make this many stacks:
Over 14"	One repeat per layer	1

Stack all layers, keeping the layers from each half-width grouped together. Adjust the second half-width as needed so that the motifs match. Pin through all 10 or 12 layers.

Whack…	To make…
(2–3) 6" strips across width	(20) wedge block kits (7–11 per strip, depending on the usable width of the stack)

Note that, because of normal variations in printing, it may be more difficult to match these repeats accurately. Patience and careful pinning will help.

Running 'Round in Circles

Running 'Round in Circles

Finished Block Size: 20"
Finished Quilt Top: 88" x 88"
Wedge Size: 8"
Wedge Type Shown: 18° (20 per circle)

A scrap lovers dream! Bright novelty prints combine with black and white background fabrics in this exuberant design.

Fabric Requirements
Measurements in yards unless otherwise indicated.

If the design repeat of **Main Fabric** is	7"–10"	11"–14"	15"–17"	18"–26"	over 26"
You will need this many yards for the Stack-n-Whack version: with 18°, 20-wedge circles	9¼	8⅝	10½	8	10 repeats
with 15°, 24-wedge circles	11	10⅜	12½	9⅝	12 repeats
Or, for strip-cut or scrap fan wedges	4¾ yds. or equivalent in scraps*				

Additional Fabrics	
Background Fabric	5½ or equivalent in assorted fabrics
Accent Fabric (bias-edge trim and cornerstone appliqué)	2
Accent Fabric (block center circles)	¼*
Inner Border	⅜
Outer Border	2¾ (seamless) or 1⅛ (pieced)
Backing (3 panels pieced lengthwise)	8⅛
Binding (cut 2½" strip crosswise)	⅞
*Selective cutting may require more yardage.	

Cutting Stack-n-Whack Wedges

Prepare the main fabric, following the directions on pages 23–29.

Stack-n-Whack Chart for Running 'Round in Circles

Cut layers 21" wide. Cut 10 identical layers for 18° fans, or 12 identical layers for 15° fans.
Use a different set of identical repeats for each additional stack.

If the lengthwise design repeat is:	Use this many design repeats:	Make this many stacks:
6" – 10"	Three repeats per layer	2
11" – 18"	Two repeats per layer	2
Over 18"	One repeat per layer	2

Whack…	To make…
(4) 8" strips across width	(32) wedge block kits (8–9 per strip). You will use two block kits for each circle.

Cutting Strip-Cut or Scrap Wedges

Cut 8" wedges from assorted fabrics, following the instructions starting on page 20. You will need (320) 18° wedges for 20-wedge circles or (384) 15° wedges for 24-wedge circles.

Cutting the Background Fabric

From one or more background fabrics, cut (16) 20½" squares.

Making the Blocks

Piece 16 full-circle fans, using your choice of techniques.

For the Stack-n-Whack version, use two sets of 10 or 12 wedges for each circle, alternating the wedges (Figure 2–27, page 114).

For the bias-edge trim around the large circles, as seen in the quilt photo, cut (2) 22" strips across the width of the accent fabric. From these, cut 1¼" bias strips and piece as necessary to make (16) 59" strips. See page 34 for instructions on applying the trim. Appliqué the fans to the 16 background fabric squares. Prepare (16) 3" circles (pattern on page 133) for the block centers, and appliqué the center circles in place.

Assembling the Quilt Top

Arrange the blocks, following the quilt assembly diagram (Figure 2–28, page 114). Sew the vertical seams in each row, then sew the rows together.

FIGURE 2-27. Stack-n-Whack version.

Adding Appliquéd Cornerstones

The small circles in between the wedge circles are appliquéd in layers, with a white four-patch circle on top of a larger black circle. For the bottom layer, make (9) 5" circles, (12) 5" half-circles, and (4) 5½" quarter-circles (circle patterns on page 133).

For the four-patch circles, cut (60) 3" squares of background fabric. Piece (9) four-patch units and use these to make 4½" circles. Piece (12) two-patch units to make 4½" half-circles. Make (1) 5" circle and cut it into quarters.

Appliqué the top circles to the base circles, then appliqué the base circles to the quilt top, centering them on the seam intersections between the blocks.

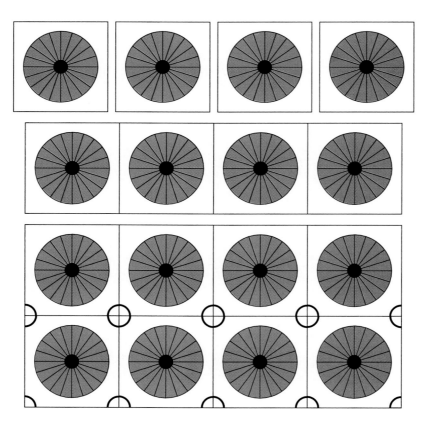

FIGURE 2-28. Quilt assembly.

Adding the Borders

From the inner border fabric, cut (8) 1" strips across the width from the border accent fabric, and piece in pairs to make 4 long strips. From the outer border fabric, cut (9) 4" strips across the width and piece to make one long strip, or cut (4) 4" x 90" lengthwise strips.

Measure the quilt top down the center and cut two inner borders this length. Sew the borders to two opposite sides.

Measure across the width in the center of the quilt, including borders, and cut two inner borders this length. Sew them to the top and bottom.

Measure, cut, and sew the outer border in the same fashion.

What if...

I use batiks for the wedges?

Scrap fabrics, including batiks, make wonderful wedge circles (Figure 2–29).

FIGURE 2-29. Batik wedge circle block.

Tri-Fangles

Tri-Fangles

Finished Block Size: 10¾" x 12½"
Finished Quilt Top: 56" x 62"
Wedge Length: 9"
Wedge Type: 15° (4 per fan)

Fabric Requirements
Measurements in yards unless otherwise indicated.

If the design repeat of **Main Fabric A** is	6"–10"	11"–14"	15"–17"	18"–26"	over 26"
You will need this many yards for the Stack-n-Whack version	2½	1⅞	2¼	3¼	4 repeats
Or, for strip-cut or scrap fan wedges	1¼ yds. or equivalent in scraps				
Additional Fabrics					
Background	3⅜				
Accent (bias-edge finish)	⅜				
Optional Border Accent Strip	¼				
Border*	1⅞ (seamless) or ¾ (pieced)				
Backing (pieced lengthwise)	4				
Binding (cut 2½ " strips crosswise)	⅝				

*For repeats over 18" only, the Main Fabric yardage for the Stack-n-Whack version includes the border. If you would like to use a different fabric, this is the extra yardage you will need, but don't reduce the Main Fabric yardage.

Cutting Stack-n-Whack Wedges

Prepare the main fabric, following the directions on pages 23–29.

Stack-n-Whack Chart for Tri-Fangles
Cut layers 21" wide. Cut 4 identical layers for 15° fans.
Use a different set of identical repeats for each additional stack.

If the lengthwise design repeat is:	Use this many design repeats:	Make this many stacks:
6" – 10"	Two repeats per layer	2
11" – 18"	One repeat per layer	2
Over 18"	One repeat per layer	1
Whack…		**To make…**
(2) 9" strips across the width		(18) wedge block kits (9 per strip)

Cutting Strip-Cut or Scrap Wedges

Cut 9" wedges, following the instructions on page 21. You will need (72) 15° wedges.

Cutting Background Fabric	
First Cut	**Second Cut**
(9) 11½" strips across width	(35) 60° triangles and 5 pairs of side triangles, using the following instructions.

Cutting Background Triangles

The background triangles for the fans and setting triangles will be cut from 60° diamonds. To make the diamonds, fold the 11½" background strips in half with selvages together. Place the 60° line of the ruler on one edge of the strip, far enough in to avoid the selvages, and cut as shown in Figure 2–30.

To cut the other side of the diamond, you will need a second ruler, which can be square or rectangular, as long as it is at least 11½" in one dimension. Place the second ruler on the fabric so that its 11½" line is on the angled cut edge. Butt the first ruler against the second, as shown in Figure 2–31, page 120, and place the 60° line on the bottom edge of the strip. Hold the first ruler in place, nudge the second ruler out of the way, then cut the 60° angle to complete the diamond.

To cut the diamonds into 60° triangles, place the 60° line on one edge and cut from corner to corner (Figure 2–32, page 120).

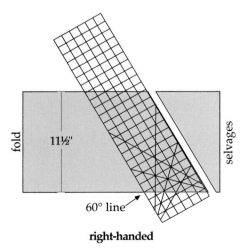

fold   11½"   selvages

60° line

right-handed

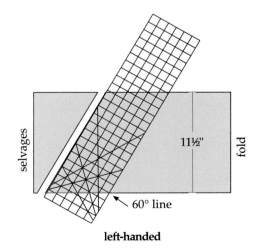

selvages   11½"   fold

60° line

left-handed

Figure 2–30. First cut a 60° diamond.

Cut the side triangles from the remaining strips at the fold: Turn the folded piece so that the triangle base is at the top, as shown in Figure 2–33. Align one of the crosswise lines of the ruler with the base of the triangle. Place the ruler's ½" line so that it crosses the corner at the lower edge of the triangle, as shown. Trim away the folded edge.

You now have a pair of side triangles, one A and one B (Figure 2–34). Make a total of 5 A triangles and 5 B triangles in this manner.

Making the Blocks

Piece 18 fans, using your choice of techniques. Bias-edge finishing was used for the fans in the quilt photo. For bias-edge finish, cut an 8½" strip across the width of the accent fabric. Cut (18) 1¼" bias strips. Appliqué the fans to the background triangles.

For the fused semi-circle bases shown, use the 3½" circle on page 133. Trace the circle three times on paper-backed fusible web, including the 30° cutting lines. Fuse the web

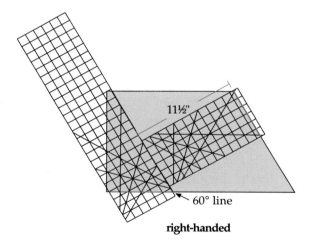

right-handed   left-handed

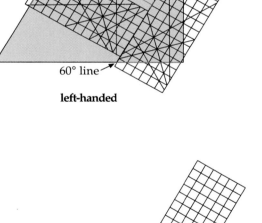

Figure 2-31. Finish cutting the diamond.

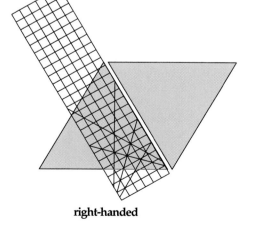

right-handed

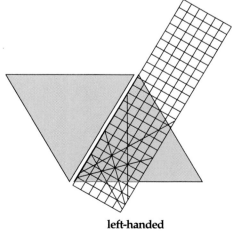

left-handed

Figure 2-32. Cut diamond to make two triangles.

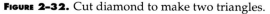

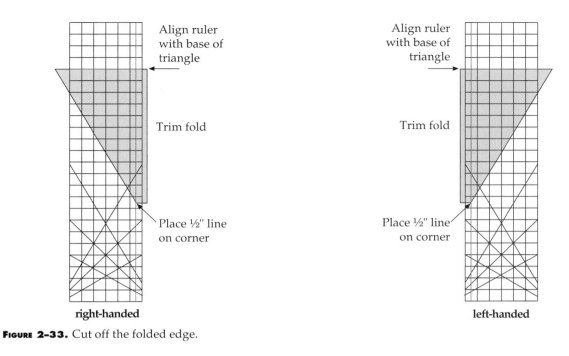

FIGURE 2-33. Cut off the folded edge.

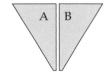

FIGURE 2-34. A pair of side triangles.

to the wrong side of the base fabric and cut out the circles. Cut apart each circle to make (6) 30° fan bases. Appliqué the bases to the fan blocks.

Assembling the Quilt Top

Arrange the fan blocks and setting triangles, following the quilt assembly diagram (Figure 2–35). Sew the diagonal seams in each row, then sew the rows together.

Cut (2) 2" strips across the width from the remaining background fabric. Piece them together to make one long strip. Measure across the width in the center of the quilt, and cut the strip to this length. Sew the strip to the bottom of the quilt.

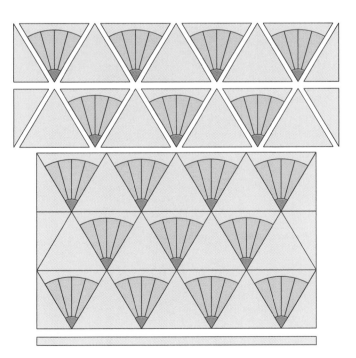

FIGURE 2-35. Quilt assembly.

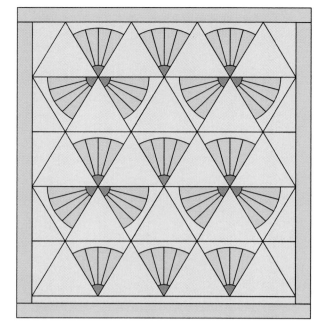

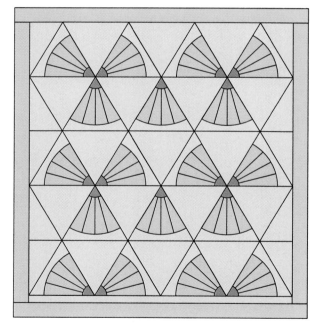

FIGURE 2–36. Tri-Fangles variations.

Optional Folded Border Accent

For the optional border insert strip, cut (6) 1¼" strips across the width. Piece the strips together on the diagonal, as for binding. Press the pieced strip in half lengthwise, right side out.

Measure the length of the quilt down the center and cut two insert strips this length. Using a scant ¼" seam allowance, machine baste the strips to the long sides, matching the raw edges.

Measure across the width in the center of the quilt and cut two strips this length. Baste them to the two remaining sides, overlapping the other strips at the corners.

Adding the Borders

The borders have butted corners. Cut (6) 3½" strips across the width and piece them to make one long strip, or cut (4) 3½" x 58" lengthwise strips.

Measure the quilt top down the center and cut two borders this length. Sew the borders to two opposite sides.

Measure across the width in the center of the quilt, including borders, and cut two borders this length. Sew them to the two remaining sides.

What if...

I rotate the blocks?

Rotating the blocks can create delightful new designs (Figure 2–36).

Floating Fans

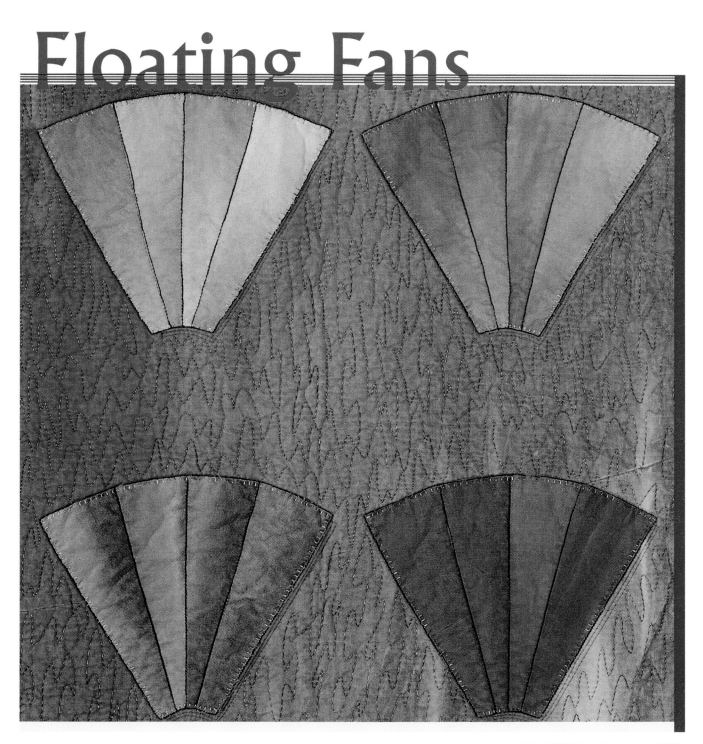

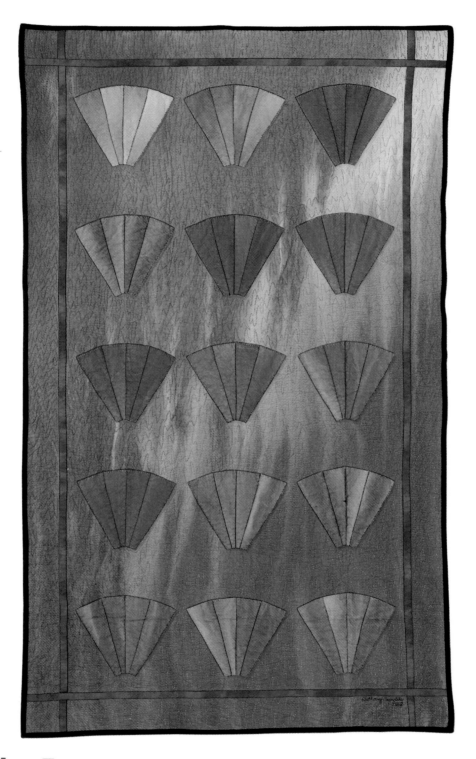

Floating Fans

Finished Quilt Top: 32" x 56"

Wedge Length: 6"

Wedge Type: 15° (4 per fan)

A beautiful length of hand-dyed cotton provides both background and fan wedges for this quilt. Yardages are given separately here so that you can use your own special combination. A narrow pieced-in border frames the fans without interrupting the background design.

Fabric Requirements
Measurements in yards unless otherwise indicated.

If the design repeat of **Main Fabric A** is	7"–10"	11"–14"	15"–17"	18"–26"	over 26"
You will need this many yards for the Stack-n-Whack version	1⅜	1⅞	2¼	3¼	4 repeats
Or, for strip-cut or scrap fan wedges	⅝ yd. or equivalent in scraps				
Additional Fabrics					
Background	1¾				
Border Insert	¼				
Backing (pieced lengthwise)	1¾				
Binding (cut 2½" strips crosswise)	½				

Preparing Background and Insert

From the background fabric, cut a panel 32" x 56". From the border insert fabric, cut (5) 1" strips across the width. Piece together three of the strips to make one long strip. From the long strip, cut (2) 56" strips for the sides of the quilt. Cut the remaining strips to 32" for the top and bottom.

To insert the strips, cut a 3" strip from each long side of the 32" x 56" panel. Sew the 1" x 56" inserts to the two long sides of the panel. Press seam allowances toward the inserts. Sew the 3" background strips to the insert strips, making sure to orient them correctly if there is an obvious pattern to the background fabric. Press seam allowances toward the inserts.

Cut a 3" strip from the top and from the bottom of the panel, cutting through the inserts. Sew the 1" x 32" strips to the top and bottom of the panel and press seam allowances toward the inserts. Sew the 3" background strips to the inserts, matching seams at the corner intersections. Press seam allowances toward the inserts. The quilt top should still measure 32" x 56".

Cutting Stack-n-Whack Wedges

Prepare the main fabric, following the directions on pages 23–29.

Stack-n-Whack Chart for Floating Fans		
Cut layers 21" wide. Cut 4 identical layers for 15° fans. Use a different set of identical repeats for each additional stack.		
If the lengthwise design repeat is:	**Use this many design repeats:**	**Make this many stacks:**
7" – 13"	One repeat per layer	2
Over 13"	One repeat per layer	1
Whack…		**To make…**
(2) 6" strips across the width		(15) wedge block kits (8 per strip)

Strip-Cut or Scrap Version

Cut (60) 15°, 6" wedges, following the instructions starting on page 20. Note that the fans in the quilt photo are raw-edge machine appliquéd. If you prefer to press under a ¼" seam on all sides of the fan, cut 6¾" or 7" wedges.

Piecing and Appliquéing the Fans

Piece 15 fans, as described on page 29.

Press the background panel in quarters to mark the center lines. Using a temporary marker, such as chalk, establish a base line 3" below the horizontal center fold. Refer to Figure 2–38 to measure and mark the rest of the fan placement guidelines on the background fabric.

Pin or spray-baste the fans to the background panel, aligning the center seam of each fan with a vertical placement line, and the lower edge with a horizontal line. Stitch the fans in place with a machine blanket stitch or satin stitch.

What if…

I have a different size background or my fans want to play outside the lines?

Experiment! The only rules for this layout are the ones you set yourself (Figure 2–39).

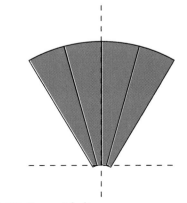

FIGURE 2–37. Fan guide lines.

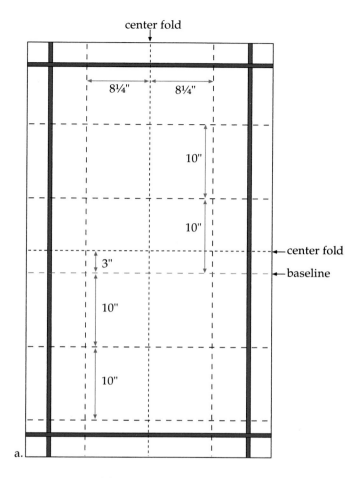

center fold

8¼"   8¼"

10"

10"

center fold

3"   baseline

10"

10"

a.

FIGURE 2-38. (a) Fan placement guide lines. (b) Fans in place.

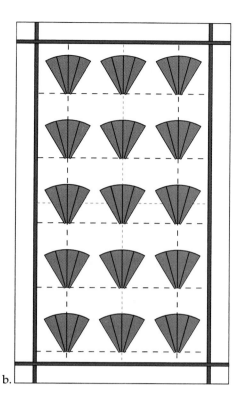

b.

FIGURE 2-39. Floating Fans variation.

Kyoto Fans

Machine quilted by Diane Thomas, Columbia Falls, Montana.

Kyoto Fans

Finished Quilt Top: 93" x 102"
Wedge Length: 9"
Wedge Type: 15° (8 per fan)

Fabric Requirements
Measurements in yards unless otherwise indicated.

If the design repeat of **Main Fabric A** is	6"–10"	11"–14"	15"–17"	18"–27"	over 27"
You will need this many yards for the Stack-n-Whack version	5	3½	4¼	6⅜	8 repeats
Or, for strip-cut or scrap fan wedges	2¼ yds. or equivalent in scraps				
Additional Fabrics					
Background	7⅜				
First and Third Borders	3 (seamless) or 1¾ (pieced)				
Second Border*	2¾ (seamless) or 1⅜ (pieced)				
Backing (pieced lengthwise)	9				
Binding (cut 2½" strips crosswise)	⅞				

*For repeats over 18" only, the Main Fabric yardage for the Stack-n-Whack version includes the border. If you would like to use a different fabric, this is the extra yardage you will need, but don't reduce the Main Fabric yardage.

Cutting Stack-n-Whack Wedges

Prepare the main fabric, following the directions on pages 23–29.

Stack-n-Whack Chart for Kyoto Fans
Cut layers 21" wide. Cut 8 identical layers for 15° fans.
Use a different set of identical repeats for each additional stack.

If the lengthwise design repeat is:	Use this many design repeats:	Make this many stacks:
6"-10"	Two repeats per layer	2
11"–18"	One repeat per layer	2
Over 18"	One repeat per layer	1

Whack...	To make...
(2) 9" strips across width	(18) wedge block kits (9 per strip)

Cutting Strip-Cut or Scrap Wedges

Cut (144) 9", 15° wedges, following the instructions starting on page 20.

Cutting Background Fabric	
First Cut	**Second Cut**
(14) 11½" strips across width	(28) 60° diamonds and (7) pairs of side triangles, following the instructions on pages 119–120, *except do not cut* the diamonds into triangles.
(1) 13" x 80" lengthwise strip	(3) 2½" x 80" top and side setting strips, and (1) 4½" x 80" bottom setting strip.
From the remaining width (approximately 29"), cut:	
(7) 11½" strips across width	(7) 60° diamonds (one diamond from each unfolded strip).

Making the Fans

Piece 18 fans, using your choice of techniques. The fans in the quilt photo are finished with fusible bias trim (page 39). Appliqué the fans to the background diamonds.

Assembling the Quilt Top

Arrange the fan blocks and the setting diamonds and triangles, following the quilt assembly diagram (Figure 2–40). Sew the diagonal seams in each row, then sew the rows together.

Measure the quilt top down the center and cut two of the 2½" x 80" strips of background fabric to this length. Sew the borders to the sides of the quilt.

Measure across the width in the center of the quilt, including the background strips, and cut the remaining background fabric strips to this length. Sew the 2½"-wide strip to the top of the quilt and the 4½"-wide strip to the bottom.

Figure 2–40. Quilt assembly.

Adding the Borders

The borders have butted corners. For the first and third borders, cut (18) 3" strips across the width and piece them to make one long strip, or cut (4) 3" x 85" and (4) 3" x 99" lengthwise strips.

For the second border, cut (9) 5" strips across the width and piece them to make one long strip, or cut (4) 5" x 90" lengthwise strips.

Measure the quilt top down the center and cut two strips this length for the first border. Sew the borders to the two opposite sides.

Measure across the width in the center of the quilt, including borders, and cut two borders this length. Sew them to the two remaining sides. Repeat for the second and third borders.

What if...

I'd like to make this in a throw size?

For a throw-size, Stack-n-Whack version (Figure 2–41), use the same main fabric yardages, but reduce the background fabric to 3¼ yards and the accent fabric to ¾ yard.

For the main fabric, you will need only (1) 9" strip for the 8 fans.

Cut (15) background diamonds and (5) sets of side triangles from (8) 11½" strips.

Cut (3) 2½" and (1) 4½" strips across the width for the background setting strips.

Cut (6) 3" strips for the first border and piece them in one long strip before cutting to length. Use the remaining half-width of the main fabric for the second border.

FIGURE 2–41. Kyoto Fans variation.

wedge and circle patterns

circle templates

See page 18 for instructions on using templates.

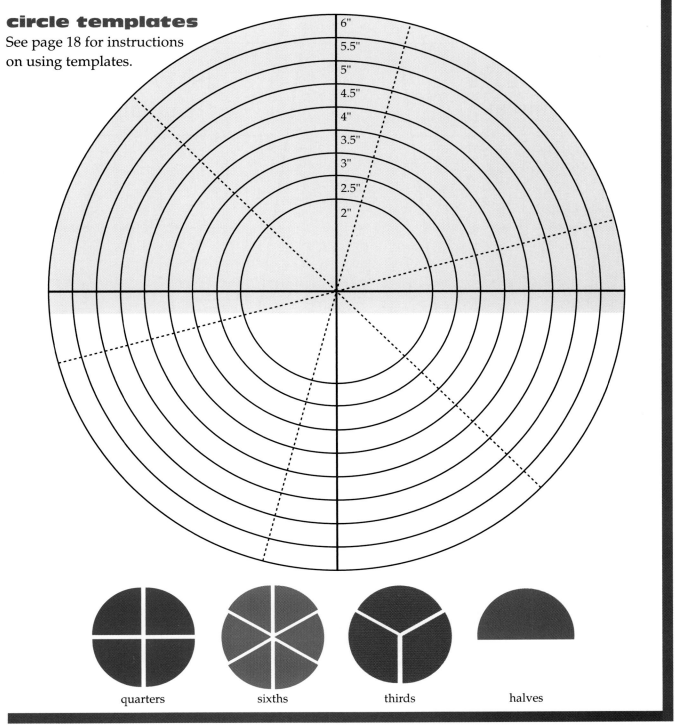

6"
5.5"
5"
4.5"
4"
3.5"
3"
2.5"
2"

quarters sixths thirds halves

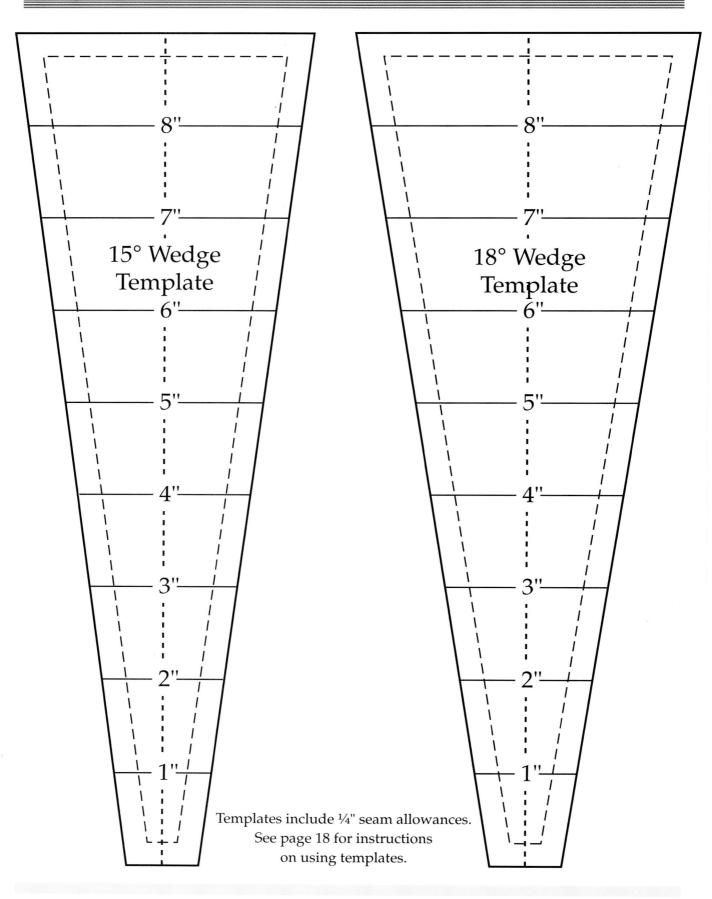

15° Wedge Template

8"

7"

6"

5"

4"

3"

2"

1"

18° Wedge Template

8"

7"

6"

5"

4"

3"

2"

1"

Templates include ¼" seam allowances.
See page 18 for instructions
on using templates.

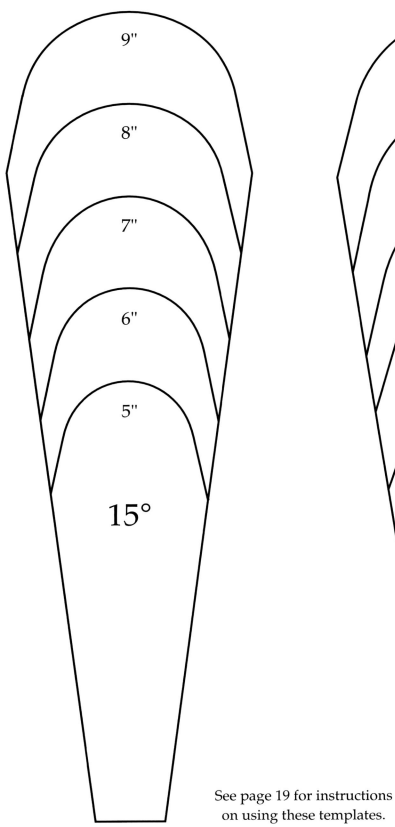

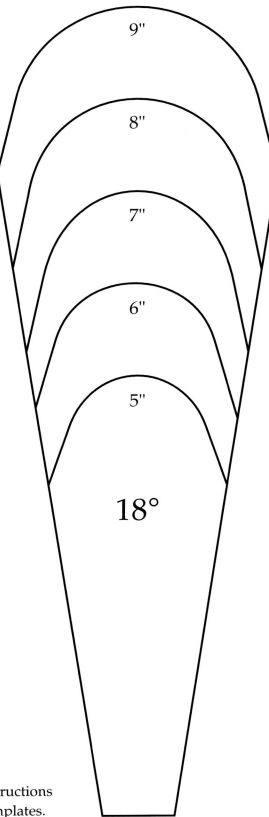

9"

8"

7"

6"

5"

15°

18°

See page 19 for instructions
on using these templates.

reference tables

How to Read a Stack-n-Whack Chart

While the number of layers and the shapes to cut will vary depending on the design, the stacking process is the same for all projects. Understanding the Stack-n-Whack chart (sample on page 137) is a key step in using these patterns successfully.

Use the top part of the chart, sections A–D, to cut the layers for your stack. After the layers have been stacked, refer to the bottom of the chart, sections E and F, for the whacking instructions.

Top of Chart

Section A. At the top of the chart, you will find the information on the crosswise measurement of the stack and the number of layers needed for each stack. Most projects call for a 21" width, or about half the crosswise (selvage to selvage) width if the fabric is 42" wide. This width allows for easy and efficient cutting with a 24" ruler. Some projects specify a narrower width to conserve uncut fabric. The number of layers depends on the number of identical pieces needed for each block.

Section B. The first column divides fabric prints into two or more groups, depending on the length of the design repeat. See page 23 for directions on finding this measurement.

Section C. The second column shows how many design repeats to use for each layer, depending on the repeat length. This number of repeats will make the stack long enough to cut the block pieces efficiently.

Section D. The third column shows the number of stacks needed. If you need to make a second stack, use the remaining width of the fabric. Be sure to use a different part of the design for the second stack.

Bottom of Chart

Section E. The left column tells the total number of strips (in parentheses) to cut from one or more stacks and the width of the strips. Strips are cut crosswise, from the selvage to the torn edge.

Section F. The right column lists the total number of block kits to cut.

Sample Stack-n-Whack Chart		
A Cut layers 21" wide. Cut 5 identical layers for 18° fans, or 6 identical layers for 15° fans. Use a different set of identical repeats for each additional stack.		
If the lengthwise design repeat is:	**Use this many design repeats:**	**Make this many stacks:**
6" – 10"	Three repeats per layer	2
11" – 18"	Two repeats per layer	2
Over 18"	One repeat per layer	2
E Whack...	**F** To make...	
(4) 8" strips across width	(32) wedge block kits (8–9 per strip)	

Top of chart

Bottom of chart

Average Number of Wedges per Strip

Yield may vary depending on the width of the fabric, width of the selvage, and cutting accuracy.

Strip/Wedge Size	21" strip (half-width)		42" strip (full-width)	
	18° Wedges	15° Wedges	18° Wedges	15° Wedges
5"	11	13	25	27
6"	11	11	23	25
7"	9	9	21	23
8"	9	9	19	21
9"	8	9	17	19

On-Point Setting

Finished Block Size	5"	6"	7"	8"	9"	10"	11"	12"
Finished diagonal measurement	7⅛"	8½"	10"	11⅜"	12¾"	14¼"	15⅝"	17"
Cut size for background and alternate squares	5½"	6½"	7½"	8½"	9½"	10½"	11½"	12½"
Cut square size for side triangles. Cut each square twice on the diagonal to make 4 triangles.	8⅜"	9¾"	11¼"	12⅝"	14"	15½"	16⅞"	18¼"
Cut square size for corner triangles. Cut each square once on the diagonal to make 2 triangles.	4½"	5⅛"	5⅞"	6⅝"	7¼"	8"	8¾"	9⅜"

lesson plans

Teachers and shop owners are welcome to develop classes with this book as a textbook. Please remember that the book's copyright prohibits photocopying or other printing of any materials herein, with the exception of the templates on pages 133–135, which may be copied for personal use only. The following suggestions for lesson plans will fit various class schedules.

Three-Hour Class

Stack-n-Whack version: Students bring the main fabric only. To minimize cutting and pressing time, have students make five-wedge fan blocks. They can make a stack, cut block kits, and begin piecing the fans, using one combination of piecing and edge finishing techniques. Demonstrate the remaining steps for appliquéing the blocks and discuss the setting and finishing steps.

Scrap version: Students bring background fabric and a variety of scrap fabrics. Students can learn one combination of piecing and edge finishing techniques, and complete several blocks. Discuss setting and finishing steps.

Six-Hour Class

For intermediate level classes, students can cut some of the background fabric before class.

Stack-n-Whack version: Students bring the main fabric and any additional fabrics needed to piece the blocks. They can make one stack, cut block kits and piece several blocks, using one combination of piecing and edge finishing techniques. Recommended projects—FLIP-FLOP FANS, FLOURISHING FANS, VERY VICTORIAN, RAINBOWS & RICKRACK, TRI-FANGLES, LAZY DAISIES.

Scrap version: Students bring a variety of scraps, along with background and accent fabric. They can learn one combination of piecing and edge finishing techniques, and complete several blocks. Recommended Projects—scrap versions of any of the recommended patterns in the Stack-n-Whack version, plus SUGAR & SPICE, REDWORK RIBBONS, and RUNNING 'ROUND IN CIRCLES.

Two Three-Hour Classes

This format gives students the option of piecing the fans or circles before selecting the background fabric. Recommended projects—any of the Stack-n-Whack fan designs, including the FAN SAMPLER.

Session 1: Students cut the block kits, learning the Stack-n-Whack method, and begin piecing the fan or circle units. Optional: demonstrate or have students try additional piecing and finishing techniques. Allow time at the end of class to preview background fabrics.

Session 2: Students appliqué their pieced units to the background fabric and may begin setting the blocks together.

Four Two to Three-Hour Classes

This longer format allows more time for help with fabric selection and other design decisions. For an introductory level class, teach one combination of piecing and edge finishing techniques and suggest a specific layout. For intermediate and advanced students, cover additional techniques and offer more flexibility in design choices. Recommended projects—Any of the Stack-n-Whack fan or circle designs, including FAN SAMPLER, FULL PLATES, and KYOTO FANS.

Session 1: Present a variety of piecing and finishing techniques, and have students try out their favorites with scrap fabric. Discuss fabric selection for Stack-n-Whack projects, including mirror-image options and symmetrical fabrics if desired. Students should select the wedge fabric and accent fabric, if needed, before the second session.

Session 2: Students cut the block kits, learning the Stack-n-Whack method, and begin piecing the fan or circle units using their choice of techniques. Allow time at the end of class to preview background fabrics.

Session 3: Students appliqué their pieced units to the background fabric. Discuss setting options.

Session 4: Assemble the quilt. Discuss quilting and finishing techniques.

bibliography

Stack-n-Whack® techniques and designs

Reynolds, Bethany S. *Magic Stack-n-Whack® Quilts*. Paducah, Ky.: American Quilter's Society, 1998.

——. *Stars a la Carte*. Paducah, Ky.: American Quilter's Society, 2000.

——. *Stack-n-Whackier Quilts*. Paducah, Ky.: American Quilter's Society, 2001.

Machine quilting techniques

Gaudynski, Diane. *Guide to Machine Quilting*. Paducah, Ky.: American Quilter's Society, 2002.

Noble, Maurine. *Machine Quilting Made Easy*. Bothell, Wash.: That Patchwork Place, 1994.

Noble, Maurine, and Elizabeth Hendricks. *Machine Quilting with Decorative Threads*. Bothell, Wash.: That Patchwork Place, 1994.

sources

BSR Design, Inc.

P.O. Box 1374
Ellsworth, ME 04605
website: www.bethanyreynolds.com

Patterns, Stack-n-Whack® rulers and Circle Buddies template set for marking and pressing fabric circles; workshops and lectures with Bethany Reynolds

eQuilter.com

5455 Spine Road, Suite E
Boulder, CO 80301
website: www.equilter.com

Online retailer; quilt fabrics and notions, including fusible bias tape and Synthrapol® detergent additive

J.T. Trading Corporation

P.O. Box 9439
Bridgeport, CT 06601-9439
(203) 339-4904

Basting spray for appliqué and quilting; wool batting

PineTree Quiltworks

585 Broadway
South Portland, ME 04106
(207) 799-7357
website: www.quiltworks.com

Quilting fabrics and supplies, including patterns and rulers by Bethany Reynolds

Quilted by Diane

Diane Thomas
PO Box 204B
Columbia Falls, MT 59912-2048
(406) 892-2625

Custom machine quilting services

about the author

Bethany Reynolds has been quilting and teaching since 1982. Before they became parents, Beth and her husband, Bill, owned a fabric and quilt shop for 10 years. Beth says, "Because I personally dislike finicky stuff, like set-in seams and curved piecing, I've always put a lot of my energy into devising easier ways to get great results. Thanks to the popularity of the Stack-n-Whack® method, I've had the opportunity to share my designs and tricks with quilters across the United States, as well as in Australia, England, and France. For a girl who grew up on a Maine island, this has been an exciting adventure and a good geography lesson!"

Bethany still lives on the coast of Maine with her son and her husband, who manages their ruler and pattern business. She spends about a quarter of her time traveling and teaching. At home, besides quilting, Beth enjoys cooking, computer graphics, reading, and downhill skiing.

Author of *Magic Stack-n-Whack®*, *Stars a la Carte*, and *Stack-n-Whackier*.

other AQS books

This is only a small selection of the books available from the American Quilter's Society. AQS books are known worldwide for timely topics, clear writing, beautiful color photos, and accurate illustrations and patterns. The following books are available from your local bookseller, quilt shop, or public library.

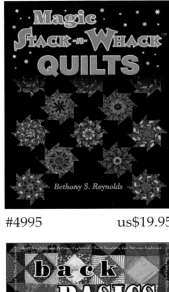

#4995   us$19.95

#5850   us$21.95

#5589   us$21.95

#6293   us$24.95

#5755   us$21.95

#6076   us$21.95

#6210   us$24.95

#6079   us$21.95

#6074   us$21.95

LOOK for these books nationally, **CALL** or **VISIT** our website at www.AQSquilt.com   **1-800-626-5420**